Tracing the Rainbow
Through the Rain

Tracing the Rainbow Through the Rain

O. S. Hawkins

BROADMAN PRESS
Nashville, Tennessee

Unless otherwise indicated, all Scripture references are from the King James
Version of the Holy Bible. All Scripture references marked NASB are from the
New American Standard Bible. © Copyright The Lockman Foundation, 1960,
1962, 1963, 1968, 1971, 1972, 1973, 1975, 1977. Used by permission.

Dewey Decimal Classification: 248.4
Subject Heading: CHRISTIAN LIFE
Printed in the United States of America

Library of Congress Cataloging in Publication Data

Hawkins, O. S.
    Tracing the rainbow through the rain.

    1. Consolation—Sermons. 2. Baptists—Sermons.
3. Southern Baptist Convention—Sermons. 4. Sermons,
American. I. Title.
BV4905.2.H39 1985   248.4'86106   85-6610
ISBN 0-8054-5020-3

Dedication

To Susie ...

... Who said to me on July 24, 1970, "Wherever you go I'll go, wherever you lodge I'll lodge, your people shall be my people, and your God shall be my God." And she has kept that promise.

... She has lived with me in a little "lean-to" house in Fort Worth, in the beautiful parsonages in Oklahoma, and finally in our own home in Florida.

... I am thankful to her parents, Don and Nelle, who one night while tucking their ten-year-old daughter into bed planted a seed by saying, "Maybe someday God will let you marry a preacher!"

... In a very real sense she is my own pastor, my counselor, and beyond that—my very best friend.

... Thank you, Susie, for always being there, *Tracing the Rainbow Through the Rain.*

About the Author

Dr. O. S. Hawkins is pastor of the First Baptist Church, Fort Lauderdale, Florida, where he has served since 1978. His church is known internationally for its evangelism and ministry to human needs. The church baptizes between 500 and 1,000 persons a year, and ministers to people from all walks of life. Each year at Thanksgiving the church has a feast for 3,000 or more.

Dr. Hawkins is a native of Fort Worth, Texas. He married the former Susan Kay Cavness of Austin on July 24, 1970. They have two daughters, Wendy and Holly. The Hawkins family enjoys travel and outdoor recreation together, including golf and fishing.

Hawkins graduated from Polytechnic High School, Texas Christian University (B.B.A.), and Southwestern Baptist Theological Seminary (M.Div.), all in Fort Worth. He was honored with the doctor of sacred theology degree from Southwest Baptist University at Bolivar, Missouri, and with the doctor of divinity degree from Dallas Baptist University, Dallas, Texas.

Before coming to Fort Lauderdale, he was pastor of First Baptist Church, Ada, Oklahoma (1974-1978), First Baptist Church, Hobart, Oklahoma (1972-1974), and assistant pastor at Sagamore Hill Baptist Church, Fort Worth (1969-1972).

He is on television across the nation and has published five books with Broadman—this one, *When Revival Comes* (with Jack R. Taylor), *After Revival Comes, Clues to a Successful Life*, and *Where Angels Fear to Tread*.

Acknowledgments

I am indebted to a number of people who, in their own unique and diversified ways, have made this volume a reality.

My friends at Broadman Press ... From the beginning of our relationship five books ago, they have encouraged and helped me every step of the way.

Wendy and Holly ... They have allowed their Dad time in the evenings to study and write. As God has enlarged our personal ministry, they have never complained about sharing me with others. I am awfully proud to be their Dad!

Pete Cantrell of Ada, Oklahoma ... The eternal optimist! He sees a rainbow in every rainstorm and taught me years ago to look for the silver lining.

Jack R. Taylor ... who "got me started" when we collaborated on *When Revival Comes*. But more importantly he taught me to walk with God as we walked around the walls of Jerusalem late one night.

Dr. R. T. Kendall ... who stimulates my thinking like no one else. This great pastor of Westminster Chapel in London has a heart for revival like few men I know. While we were vacationing together last summer, R. T. asked, "Why don't you call the book *Tracing the Rainbow Through the Rain?*"

David Hamilton ... and all our staff at First Baptist Church of Fort Lauderdale. They "make it happen" in our personal Jerusalem. Thank you, David, for standing faithfully by my side for over ten years now.

Wanda Todd ... my super secretary. This volume, like the ones before, could not have been a reality without her loyalty and creativity. She is not just a typist or secretary—she has bathed each word of this book in prayer.

Finally the Fellowship of Believers ... at the First Baptist Churches at Hobart, Oklahoma; Ada, Oklahoma; and Fort Lauderdale, Florida, who across the years have taught me in many ways far more than I have them. It has been my joy to watch them practice what I preach as they have been *Tracing the Rainbow Through the Rain.*

O. S. Hawkins

Foreword

O. S. Hawkins is one of the outstanding young pastor-evangelists in the Western World. The church he currently pastors, First Baptist Church, Fort Lauderdale, Florida, is one of the most unique churches in America. Though it is one of the largest in Florida, its ministry extends far beyond the local congregation. O. S. extensively travels. He preaches every year at the famous Westminster Chapel in London where the great G. Campbell Morgan and Martyn Lloyd-Jones ministered for many years and now has an even greater ministry under O. S. Hawkins's close friend, R. T. Kendall. Hawkins's radio, television, and writing ministry—but especially his ministry to the poor, the hurting, and the needy—have made his church famous.

Tracing the Rainbow Through the Rain is as unusual as its title. It shows the compassion, love, and understanding not only of a man well versed in psychology but in the Scriptures. I heartily commend it as a book every Christian should not only read, but study. No one can read it and be the same again!

BILLY GRAHAM
Montreat, North Carolina

Contents

1
Tracing the Rainbow Through the Rain

Tracing the Rainbow
Through the Rain

In nineteenth-century Scotland there lived a man with an amazing amount of promise and potential. He was destined for greatness, and all was going wonderfully well for him. While engaged to be married he was suddenly hospitalized. He found he had a degenerative eye disease which would eventually blind him. Consequently, his financee broke off their engagement and left him with a broken heart. George Matheson, in blindness and brokenness, within a period of five minutes, penned these hymn lyrics we believers have cherished:

O love that will not let me go
I rest my weary soul in Thee;
I give Thee back the life I owe,
That in Thine ocean depths its flow
May richer, fuller be.

O joy that seekest me through pain,
I cannot close my heart to Thee;
I trace the rainbow through the rain,
And feel the promise is not vain
That morn shall tearless be.

15

"I trace the rainbow through the rain." From the depths of despair, Matheson traced a rainbow through his personal rainstorm.

Storms of life rain on all of us. None of us are immune to these tempests of life. While writing this chapter we were involved in a tremendous storm here in downtown Fort Lauderdale. The sky grew dark, the thunder rolled, the lightning flashed, and the rain fell like lumps of lead from the sky. The palm trees bent and swayed from the gale-force winds. A few minutes later, as I looked out my office window toward the Atlantic Ocean, I beheld a gorgeous rainbow that arched across the horizon. When we spiritually keep our eyes open and gaze through the storm, we can often trace a rainbow through the rain.

As we look around our world, we view one that is freighted with violence, starvation, suffering, and disease. Wars are raging, and babies are continuing to be born with deformities. We are prone to ask, "Where is God? Why doesn't He do something? Is God really in control?"

This was the burden of the prophet Habakkuk. In fact, he begins his little Old Testament book by saying, "The burden which Habakkuk the prophet did see." In the three brief chapters making up the Book of Habakkuk, there is a marvelous progression leading us to the secret of tracing our rainbow through the rain.

In the first chapter the prophet is filled with the question "Why?" "Why doesn't God intervene? Why does God wait so long to answer prayer?"

Continuing in the second chapter, the prophet's eyes begin to perceive some marvelous answers as we hear him affirming, "The just shall live by his faithfulness." The concluding chapter finishes with a mighty crescendo of praise: "Although the fig tree shall not blossom, neither shall fruit be in the vines; the labor of the olive shall fail and the fields shall yield no meat; the flock shall be cut off from the fold, and there shall be no herd in the stalls; yet I will rejoice in the Lord, I will joy in the God of my salvation" (Hab. 3:17-18). Habakkuk had learned to trace his own rainbow through the rain.

There are three ways you and I can look at the storms of life. Some people look at the storm, and the result is confusion. Others have learned to look through the storm. That issues in confidence. But those who genuinely trace their rainbow through the rain have learned to look *beyond* the storm to find comfort. Maybe a storm is beating upon you right now—perhaps a lost job, a sickness in the family, or a lost loved one. All that many of us seem to see in the storms of life is the wind, the rain, the thunder and the lightning. But we can trace a rainbow through the rain. How? We begin by noting that:

Looking at the Storm Brings Confusion

This is what Habakkuk did. He looked at the storm and confusion set in. Listen to him as he introduces his book:

1 The burden which Habakkuk the prophet did see.
2 O Lord, how long shall I cry, and thou wilt not hear! even cry out unto thee of violence, and thou wilt not save!
3 Why dost thou show me iniquity, and cause me to behold grievance? for spoiling and violence are before me: and there are that raise up strife and contention. (Hab. 1:1-3)

He bombarded heaven with his perplexing problems. How long? Why is all this evil and suffering happening?

Habakkuk lived in a day of moral and political decay and decline. Lawlessness was rampant. Sounds familiar, doesn't it? He asked some penetrating questions, questions we all ask like "Why?" and "How long?" In chapter 1 of Habakkuk's book, God answers him: "I am sending the godless Chaldeans to destroy your city and take you captive." The truth of Scripture is: There are times when God answers us by allowing the situation to become worse before it gets better. There is a new wave of preaching today that promises all honey and no bees, no work and all ease. Some tell us if any suffering or evil befalls us it is because of sin in our lives or a lack of faith. We seldom hear these "sweetness and light" preachers preaching from a book like Habakkuk or Job. Friend, if you have a gospel which will not preach in Bangladesh, it will not preach in Fort Lauderdale or anywhere else.

Habakkuk was extremely perplexed by the horrible happenings in his world. He was having considerable difficulty reconciling what he saw with his eyes and what he believed in his heart. He was caught up in "How long?" "Why?" "It isn't fair," "It is not right," "It is not just!" The genuine problem was that Habakkuk could not understand why God was allowing all the evil and suffering to continue. "O Lord, how long shall I cry, and thou wilt not hear! even cry out unto thee of violence, and thou wilt not save!"

Habakkuk was asking what many are asking today: "If there really is a God out there Who is good and all-powerful, why doesn't He do something? Why does He allow suffering and evil? Why are there wars? Starvation? Murders? Why are babies born with deformities?"

Here is the age-old skeptical unbeliever's argument: "Either God is all-powerful but not all good (therefore He does not stop evil) or He is all-good but not all-powerful, and cannot stop evil because evil and suffering obviously continue. It all sounds so logical, doesn't it? If an all-powerful God exists, he could annihilate all evil, pain, and suffering. A God who had the power to do such would be cruel and unjust not to annihilate evil and suffering. At least, we hear that from the skeptics. As believers we affirm this omnipotent, all-powerful God. But (they tell us) He must be cruel and unjust because He doesn't stop the evils of the world.

Now, it is true that God could eradicate all evil if he wanted to do so, but think about that for a moment. Suppose that God were to decree that at midnight he was going to stamp out all evil. Many would exclaim, "Oh, that would be wonderful!" Would it? The truth is: not one of us would be here at 12:05 AM. How thankful we should be that "He hath not dealt with us after our sins; nor rewarded us according to our iniquities" (Ps. 103:10).

Mankind's general tendency is to blame God for evil and suffering. Habakkuk was doing that. How long are you going to wait? Why are you letting this happen? But the truth is God did not create evil. He created Lucifer, an angel of light in charge of praise around the throne of heaven. Lucifer made himself Satan when he decided to say "My will" instead of "Thy will be done."

People still ask, "Well, why doesn't God do something?" God *has* done something about the problem of evil. In fact, he has done the most dramatic, costly, and loving thing possible by giving his only Son to die for evil humanity! While we affirm the doctrine of divine election, which is all through the Word of God, it is also a fact that God has made us people and not puppets. The love we can voluntarily return to Him is indescribably valuable to Him. We could speculate on the origin of evil from now on, but what we must deal with is the *fact* of evil. And the only solution to the fact of evil is God's solution, which is our Lord and Savior Jesus Christ.

We can be certain that God cannot look on evil without detesting it. Habakkuk prayed to God, "Thou art of purer eyes than to behold evil, and canst not look on iniquity" (Hab. 1:13). We must learn to do what Habakkuk finally did. He carried his problem to God and left it with Him. Incidentally, this is exactly what Jesus did. As he prayed in Gethsemane's Garden, and great sweat drops of blood oozed from His skin, he cried, "Oh my Father, if it be possible let this cup pass from me; nevertheless not as I will, but as thou wilt" (Matt. 26:39). Until we take our burdens to the Lord and leave them there, we spend all of our time merely looking at the storm, which only confuses us.

If we are not careful, we will fall into this easy trap. The storm comes. Instead of looking through it or beyond it, we look at it. No wonder we become confused. Like Habakkuk, we feel trapped by our circumstances and begin to ask, "God, why don't you do something?"

As a pastor I have stood with many members (and non-members) when the storm came. I was with the Daltons when their precious baby was born with such unbelievable complications that living more than a few hours was a total impossibility. Mark and Debbie and I stood in the pediatric intensive-care unit and watched that little bundle of love breathe its last breath. Many would have looked only at the storm and known nothing but confusion, asking, "Why . . . It's just not fair!" But Mark and Debbie looked *through* the storm and found confidence. They looked beyond the storm and found comfort. They traced a rainbow through the rain!

Butch Redford was a good friend in high school. He was with me the morning I was saved. He was quite a guy, six feet six, a basketball star, and a boxing champion. When we graduated, most of our group attended college while Butch fulfilled a boyhood dream of becoming a United States Marine. One dark night in a rice paddy somewhere in South Vietnam a sniper put a bullet through his heart. Butch's blood spilled out on that faraway land. There in the darkness alone he gave up the ghost.

When we brought his body back for the funeral, one of our friends sang, "O Jesus, if I die upon a foreign field someday, t'would be no more than love demands nor less could I repay. And if by death to living the morning I shall see, I'll take my cross and follow close to thee." Many would have seen only confusion. Many would have asked, "Why? It's so useless! War doesn't make sense. How long are we going to pray and ask of God and not get an answer? Why, Butch was only nineteen years of age." But I watched his lovely family and friends look through the storm to find confidence, beyond the storm to find comfort.

One of my most heartbreaking moments was when I received

that call from Tom Elliff, my missionary friend in Zimbabwe. He and his family had left the pastorate of one of the fastest-growing churches in America to bury their lives in a distant land in the service of the Lord Jesus. He called to report that Jeannie and the children had been involved in a dreadful automobile accident on a road out in the bush. Beth, their beautiful teenage daughter, had left her friends and school where she was a cheerleader. Why? Because of the love she and her family had for the African people. Now she was in critical condition, and at best would face several years of plastic surgeries. She was at that moment in a Zimbabwe hospital where witch doctors were permitted to practice their trade freely through the corridors and rooms. Many would have looked at the storm. "Why? It's just not fair. How long is this going to go on? Lord, we've given our lives to come here and serve you." But that night on the telephone, Tom Elliff looked through the storm and found confidence, beyond the storm and found comfort. He traced a rainbow through the rain.

We as believers have never been promised lives free of difficulty and trial. "The rain falls on the just and the unjust." We all have to grapple with these questions and, like it or not, the storms come. True victory is ours when we learn to look through the storm and beyond it to trace a rainbow through the rain. Rainbows begin to appear when we realize that:

Looking Through the Storm Brings Confidence

How do we look *through* a storm? The first step is to have proper *perspective*. Habakkuk wrote, "I will stand upon my watch and set me upon the tower, and will watch to see what he will say unto me, and what I shall answer when I am reproved" (Hab. 2:1). In modern-day Israel it is not uncommon to pass through the countryside and see a watchtower. It is a stone structure where one could ascend to the top and see if the enemy were coming, where one could see the layout of the whole land. God instructed Habakkuk to go to the watchtower that he might begin to look from God's perspective at this issue of evil and suffering, and not only from his own. When we merely look from our perspective, our vision is often limited. The watchtower is an apropos place to be when asking hard questions. Habakkuk was bewildered because it appeared God wasn't doing anything in his life.

When we begin to look from God's perspective, life assumes a different dimension. Perspective is exceedingly important. The Hawkins family took a trip to Colorado sometime ago. We visited the famous Seven Falls. A natural rock formation at the top of the falls looked as if it were a covered wagon. Upon arriving there I strained to see it. Only when I had climbed two hundred steps to an observation platform across the canyon could I see the rock formation on the top of the mountain. It's impossible to see if from below, but you have a good view of it from above. It was there all the time. It's all in the perspective.

As a boy I used to play in the woods not far from our home. When we lost our way we would climb a tree in order to recover our sense of direction. This is what Habakkuk was doing. Often we are so close to the moment that we look only from our personal perspective. When we climb into the watchtower we begin to see from God's perspective.

God has a plan, and we must look at it from His perspective. We view this practically in our own daily experience. Before we take a trip, we plan our route. Before we build a house we have our blueprints of the architect's plan. We then progress through the various stages of development. So it is with God. He is never surprised by any unforeseen circumstances. All of human history is just the turning of the pages of the unfolding of God's eternal purpose and plan. He is the one "Who worketh all things after the counsel of his own will" (Eph. 1:11).

Although we do not always recognize it, God does have a plan and purpose for us. Joseph certainly found this out. Most of us know the story backwards and forwards. His brothers were so filled with hateful jealousy toward him that they sold him as a slave to the Ishmaelites who carried him away to Egypt. The brothers then lied to their father, Jacob, and told him a wild animal had slain his favorite son Joseph. Meanwhile back in Egypt, Joseph was thrown in prison because he was falsely accused, but by the time he was thirty years of age he had become the prime minister of Egypt. Consequently, he was later able to protect his family from a drastic famine.

From the human perspective, what happened to Joseph was bad. Jealousy and hatred are bad. Being separated from your father is bad; being falsely accused is bad; being in prison for thirteen years on a false charge is bad. From the human perspective, every-thing looked confusing. And yet when Joseph revealed himself to his brothers during the famine (and when he began to trace his rainbow through the rain) he testified: "Now therefore be not grieved, nor angry with yourselves, that ye sold me hither: for God did send me before you to preserve life" (Gen. 45:5). And then later he added, "You thought evil against me; but God meant it unto good" (Gen. 50:20). Yes, "We know that all things work together for good to them that love God, to them who are the called accord-ing to his purpose" (Rom. 8:28). From up in the watchtower, we begin to see from God's point of view, and we realize that some of the things seemingly meant for evil had been meant for good by God.

Habakkuk declared "watch and see what *He* will say to me." Often when the storm comes we cease to watch and wait. So we seldom hear the Lord say anything to our hearts. We're often more interested in what we say to Him or what we say to each other about Him, but the key in tracing our rainbow is to "see what He will say to me." As soon as Habakkuk carried his problem to God, he ceased to be concerned with it. If you can learn the lesson of doing that, you are almost there. The secret is to leave it there.

Perspective! The secret to the Christian life is perspective. Even bad news can sound like good news when we hear it from God's perspective. Since we seldom look from His perspective, we see Him in the blessings, but not in the afflictions where He is also present.

This is a practical lesson for us. Instead of going to everybody else and saying, "I've got a problem and don't know what to do," we need to get into the watchtower and look through the storm. "Watch and see what he will say to us." We often fail because we pray and then forget about it. After all, didn't Jesus say, "Watch and pray"? But many of us are not looking from the right perspective.

The second step in looking through the storm is *patience*. Habakkuk continued:

> 2 And the Lord answered me, and said, Write the vision and make it plain upon tables, that he may run that readeth it.
> 3 For the vision is yet for an appointed time, but at the end it shall speak, and not lie; though it tarry, wait for it; because it will surely come, it will not tarry (Hab. 2:2-3).

He now realizes the primacy of waiting on God. The person who doesn't learn patience will have trouble learning anything else. Look at Job. He lost his family, his wealth, and his health. Satan challenged God, "You've got a hedge around Job, and if he didn't have all your blessings, he wouldn't serve you." So God removed it for a purpose. When Job had lost it all, all he had left was his faith in God. Even then he wasn't sure where God was or what He was doing! Here is the acid test of discipleship—how we respond when we lose some of our blessings. Perhaps it's the loss of a job, our loved ones, or our health. Job received all kinds of unsolicited advice. In fact, his friends suggested he ought to bargain with God.

His wife said, "Curse God and die" (Job 2:9). But how did Job answer? Listen to him as he looked through his storm to find confidence, "Naked came I out of my mother's womb, and naked shall I return thither; the Lord gave and the Lord hath taken away; blessed be the name of the Lord" (Job 1:21).

How enervating it must be to wait without any seeming reason. Talk about patience—Job was filled with it. Hear him as he asserts, "Though he slay me, yet will I trust in him: but I will maintain mine own ways before him" (Job 13:15). He continues: "For I know that my Redeemer liveth and that he shall stand at the latter day upon the earth: and though after my skin worms destroy this body, yet in my flesh shall I see God: whom I shall see for myself, and mine eyes shall behold, and not another; though my reins be consumed within me" (Job 19:25-27).

When Job begins to trace his rainbow through the rain, his testimony of faith is marvelous. It lead him to say, "He knoweth the way that I take when he hath tried me, I shall come forth as gold" (Job 23:10). And later, at the end of his trial, the Bible records that "The Lord blessed the latter end of Job more than his beginning" (Job 42:12).

How many times have I heard the phrase, "It's just not fair"? And to be perfectly honest, that's a natural response for most of us. In reality it's dangerous ground when we move off the ground of grace and onto the ground of *what we think we deserve*. If God did what was "fair," I wonder where any of us would be? Listen to this man Habakkuk who came down from the watchtower: "I will stand upon my watch, and set me upon the tower, and will watch to see what he will say unto me, and what I shall answer when I am reproved. And the Lord answered me, and said, write the vision, and make it plain upon tables, that he may run that readeth it. For the vision is yet for an appointed time, but at the end it shall speak, and not lie; though it tarry, wait for it; because it will surely come, it will not tarry" (Hab. 2:1-3). Habakkuk was affirming, "I've learned something and that is patience. I am going to wait for the vision; it is certain; It cannot fail."

Friend, don't give up because the vision tarries. Don't simply look at the storm. Look through the storm, and you'll see God's perspective. You'll learn the lesson of patience, and then you'll be able to trace your rainbow through the rain.

The third step in looking through the storm is *promise*. The Bible says, "For the vision is yet for an appointed time, but at the end it shall speak, and not lie; though it tarry, wait for it; because it will surely come, it will not tarry" (Hab. 2:3). What promising words—"It will surely come!" This lesson is invaluable. What God has promised he will most assuredly perform!

If Joseph is our example of perspective and Job is our example of patience, then Joshua must be our example of promise. Those walls of Jericho were totally insurmountable. They could not be tunneled under or skirted around or climbed over! Joshua was at a loss about what to do. But then he went alone with God, started looking from God's perspective, patiently waited upon the Lord, and God gave him the promise. "The Lord said unto Joshua, See, I have given unto thine hand Jericho, and the king thereof, and the mighty men of valor. And ye shall compass the city all ye men of war, and go round about the city once. Thus shalt thou do six days. And seven priests shall bear before the ark seven trumpets of ram's horns; and the seventh day ye shall compass the city seven times, and the priests shall blow the trumpets. And it shall come to pass, that when they make a long blast with the ram's horn, and when ye hear the sound of the trumpet, all the people shall shout with a great shout; and the wall of the city shall fall down flat, and the people shall ascend up every man straight before him" (Josh. 6:2-5).

In the kingdom of God, we live by promises—not by explanations! There is no explanation for those walls of Jericho falling down flat. Yet there was the promise from God that it would happen. And though the promise tarried, it surely came to pass. None of us can fully answer all the questions of life. There must be room for faith because *what we believe always determines our behavior.*

God didn't give Naaman an explanation, but he did give him a promise. He charged him to go and dip seven times in that muddy Jordan River, and his leprosy would be cleansed. Naaman almost missed his cure because he was looking for an explanation. He was only looking at his storm and confusion had set in. Far more important than an explanation is a personal relationship with a living God. When we are deeply hurt, what we really need is not an explanation, but a revelation! A promise from God.

Cling to God's promises. Don't look at the storm. Look through the storm, and you will find confidence by looking from God's perspective and patiently waiting for his promise which will surely arrive. Then you can begin to trace your rainbow through the rain.

A fourth step in looking through the storm is *participation.* Habakkuk goes on, "Behold his soul which is lifted up is not upright in him; but the just shall live by his faith" (Hab. 2:4). Many commentators point out that this verse is more properly translated, "The just shall live by his faithfulness." This is one of the most-misquoted verses in the Bible. Many quote it as though it goes, "The just shall live by faith." But note carefully the words, "The just shall live by *his* faithfulness." The words are so simple and yet so profound.

This verse also is one of most-quoted verses in the New Testament (Rom. 1:17, Gal. 3:11, Heb. 10:38). God declares that there are only two possible attitudes in the world—faith and misguided reason (unbelief). This is the watershed. I either live my life by faith, or I live it by unbelief. Faith means living by God's word.

Note the verse carefully. I am talking about participation with Christ here. The just shall live how? "By *his faithfulness.*" When we begin to look through the storm we find this confidence in our participation with Him and in Him. Dr. R. T. Kendall, pastor of the world-famed Westminster Chapel in London, England, tells of taking his son T. R. to a new school upon their move to England. Living in a strange land and in the massive city of London, the small boy sat in fear as he rode in the car next to his father to his new school. Upon arriving at the school, T. R. would not leave the car. He simply sat there crying. Dr. Kendall lovingly said, "T. R., you go on to school and anytime during the day that you are afraid just remember that daddy will be praying for you. I am going to go home and start praying for you, and I'm going to pray for you all the day long. So anytime you are afraid, remember that your father is praying for you." T. R. climbed out of the car and never looked back. During the course of day when he was frightened, he remembered those words, and he lived that day on the strength of his father's prayers and by his father's faithfulness. This is God's message here. This is how we are to live. "The just shall live by his faithfulness."

This participation with Christ, living by His faithfulness, is what enabled those first-century Christians like Polycarp and Ignatius to face their deaths in victory. They were living by Christ's faithfulness. This was what enabled so many others when commanded to say Caesar was lord, to declare there is no Lord but Christ. "The just shall live by His faithfulness." Participation with Christ. These words transformed Martin Luther's life and ushered in the Protestant Reformation. As a Catholic monk, he was crawling on his knees up the Scala Sancta of St. Peter's at Rome in a futile attempt to be righteous through the works of penance. This verse, "The just shall live by His faithfulness," began to burn in his heart, and he ran down those steps. And all of Europe began to resound with those words: "The just shall live by His faith!"

God has promised that there will come a moment in time when no further waiting will be necessary. What a day that will be! But what do we do in the meantime? Like Habakkuk we wait patiently on the promise. Why? Because we believe God. We believe that

God is faithful! So in the meantime, and that's where we are right now, we live by his faithfulness. This is what prompted the song-writer to exult:

> Great is thy faithfulness, O God my Father
> There is no shadow of turning with Thee
> Thou changest not, Thy compassions they fail not
> As thou hast been, Thou forever wilt be.
>
> Summer and winter, and springtime and harvest
> Sun, moon and stars in their courses above
> Join with all nature in manifold witness
> To thy great faithfulness, mercy and love.
>
> Pardon for sin and a peace that endureth
> Thine own dear presence to cheer and to guide
> Strength for today and bright hope for tomorrow
> Blessings all mine, with ten thousand beside.
>
> Great is thy faithfulness
> Great is thy faithfulness
> Morning by morning new mercies I see
> All I have needed thy hand hath provided
> Great is thy faithfulness
> Lord unto me!

Habakkuk received no answers, but he was instructed how to live—"The just shall live by His faithfulness." And the wonderful outcome was—Habakkuk did what God said! We can live by His faithfulness today. Stop looking at the storm, start looking through the storm, and though the vision tarries, in the meantime partici-pate with Christ, live by His faithfulness, and you can trace your rainbow through the rain.

The fifth step in looking through the storm is *perception*. Ha-bakkuk continued in chapter 2: "The Lord is in his holy temple; let all the earth keep silence before him" (Hab. 2:20). All of the above—perspective, patience, promise, participation—led him to exclaim, "The Lord is in his holy temple." God is on the throne. He is in control. Evil may appear to triumph for a while, but that is not going to last! Its doom is sealed! God still reigns. What a perception!

This man who began in confusion, filled with questions, has now learned to look through the storm for confidence, and all this had led him to observe, "The Lord is in his holy temple." God is in control. God is yet on the throne." God is reigning, and He knows what He is doing. He will fulfill his purpose. Have you gone this far in your personal pilgrimage, or are you still looking at the storm and wallowing in your confusion? Come to the proper perception of life, and see that above it all God is still in charge.

We gaze around in our world, and it appears that the evil and worldly seem to be on top most of the time. But we need to remember that God has not abdicated His throne. He is still in His holy temple. "The way of the transgressor is hard," and everyone is going to live as long as God lives somewhere. Why does God allow it? Why does God permit all this evil and suffering? He allows it for His own purposes.

We need to remember that the Bible still avers, "And we know that all things work together for good to them that love God, to them who are the called according to his purpose" (Rom. 8:28). The Bible says, "and we know." Who knows? "*We* know," those of us who make up this family of faith. This verse is a family secret meant only for the children of God. The world certainly does not recognize the truth of Romans 8:28. The apostle says we know that "*all things* work together for good." That little word *all* is most inclusive. It entails any problem we might have. There is a crucial clause sometimes omitted from this oft-repeated verse. These things work together for good to those who are "the called according to *His purpose*." Do you realize that God has a purpose for each of us! Are you being called to His purpose?

Habakkuk started to perceive that all of this was the Lord's doing. The enemy could do nothing unless God allowed it. And if God allowed it, there must be a purpose. Habakkuk even came to perceive that as evil as the Chaldeans were, they were merely instruments in the hand of a loving Father to work His plan and His purpose in His own people. This is good medicine for us: that is, to realize that God is still on the throne. Looking from God's perspective, patiently waiting on His promise, participating with Him by living in His faithfulness, and perceiving that He is in control is how we can look through our storms.

Storms of life are inevitable; it is all in how we view them. The message of Habakkuk challenges us to cease complaining and asking "How long?" and "Why?" Find your watchtower, climb into it, and look from God's perspective in order to live by His faith. God may not plan to save you *from* your circumstances, but He will save you *through* them. Looking through the storm brings confidence, but the best means of viewing a storm is not by looking at it, or even looking through it, but to realize that:

Looking Beyond the Storm Brings Comfort

After looking through the storm in chapter 2, Habakkuk begins to look beyond the storm in chapter 3 and prays: "O Lord, I have heard thy speech, and was afraid; O Lord, revive thy work in the midst of the years, in the midst of years make known; in wrath remember mercy" (Hab. 3:2). He recalls God's faithfulness of bygone days and prays, "Lord, do it again!"

Habakkuk reminded God of what He had done in the past: "Was the Lord displeased against the rivers? Was thine anger against the rivers? Was thy wrath against the sea, that thou didst ride upon thine horses and thy chariots of salvation?" (Hab. 3:8). He remembers that just when it looked as if the Israelites were trapped at the Red Sea, Moses traced the rainbow through the rain and knew that God was on the throne. He held up the rod of God and the waters parted! "The sun and the moon stood still in their habitation; at the light of thine arrows they went, and at the shining of thy glittering spear" (Hab. 3:11). He remembered that just when it looked as if the people of God were headed for defeat, Joshua traced the rainbow through the rain, and the sun stood still until Israel won their victory. God controlled the elements. Our God can and does act! Habakkuk is reminding himself of what God had actually done. The Christian faith is solidly based on fact, not simply ideas. If the facts of the Bible are not true I have no faith or comfort. But they are true! Therefore, the prophet was looking beyond the storm and found his comfort.

Habakkuk remembered what God had done in the past and he began to cry out: "O Lord, I have heard thy speech, and was afraid; O Lord, revive thy work in the midst of years, in the midst of the years make known; in wrath remember mercy." Lord, revive Thy work. Lord, do it again!

The last verses of Habakkuk are among the richest in all the Bible. Listen to him as he reaches the crescendo of personal praise:

> Although the fig tree shall not blossom, neither shall fruit be in the vines; the labor of the olive shall fail and the fields shall yield no meat; the flock shall be cut off from the fold, and there shall be no herd in the stalls. Yet I will rejoice in the Lord, I will joy in the God of my salvation. The Lord God is my strength, and he will make my feet like hinds' feet and he will make me to walk upon mine high places" (Hab. 3:17-19).

Only the Christian can truly know what it is to rejoice in tribulation.

Habakkuk came to the point where he affirmed, "I am not going to serve God for 'what's in it for me.' But I will serve my God no matter what comes of it!" "Although the fig tree shall not blossom, neither shall fruit be in the vines; the labor of the olive shall fail, and the fields shall yield no meat, and the flock shall be cut off from the fold, and there shall be no herd in the stalls." Looking beyond the storm and finding comfort, he says, "God is my strength." Where is your strength? In your personality? In your friends? In your natural, native abilities? In your reputation? Habakkuk found his secret in knowing that his strength was in the Lord.

Note the two "I wills" of verse eighteen. "I will rejoice." "I will joy." Rejoicing and joy are only possible because of the two "He wills" in the following verse. "He will make my feet like hinds' feet. He will make me to walk upon mine high places."

Habakkuk said, "He will make my feet like hinds' feet." Like a deer's feet, swift and sure and stable he will cause me to be. Have you ever watched a deer run? He clears every obstacle so gracefully. What a contrast to the life-styles of many Christians. Instead of running like a deer on their graceful feet, many believers plod and plod and stumble and stumble.

Not only will He make me walk on hinds' feet, but He will make me walk up in the "high places." Recently while ascending Pike's Peak in a railroad car, we spotted several deer on the mountain range. They tossed their antlers in the air and swiftly sped off to the safety of high places. There the air was pure. The hunters could not reach there. Do you know these high places? Thank God for the high places in our experience of walking with Him. "I will rejoice, and I will joy in the God of my salvation." And we can do this only because "He will make me to walk on the high places." What a wonderful Savior is Jesus our Lord!

Habakkuk looked to the past, rejoicing in the victories of Joseph, Job, and Joshua. But looking from our side of Calvary, we rejoice in the fact of the resurrection. If ever there was a hopeless situation, when someone should have asked "How long?" "Why?" it was when our Lord was crucified and buried in the granite-cold dampness of Joseph's tomb. The dejected disciples went on their way. Peter said, "I am going back to the fishing business." The Emmaus disciples lamented, "We had hoped he had been the one." How long? Why? But God acted! Jesus arose! And today, He is still on the throne! That's why we sing:

> My hope is built on nothing less
> Than Jesus' blood and righteousness
> I dare not trust the sweetest frame
> But wholly lean on Jesus' name.
>
> When darkness veils His lovely face
> I rest on his unchanging grace
> In every high and stormy gale
> My anchor holds within the veil
>
> When he shall come with trumpet sound
> O may I then in him be found
> Dressed in his righteousness alone
> Faultless to stand before the throne
>
> On Christ, the solid Rock, I stand
> All other ground is sinking sand
> All other ground is sinking sand.
> —Edward Mote

But until that day God never commands us to understand. We can only trust Him and live by His faithfulness. Then when all is said and done, and we have looked beyond the storm to find comfort, we can affirm with Habakkuk, "Although the fig tree shall not blossom, neither shall fruit be in the vines; the labor of the olive shall fail, and the fields shall yield no meat; the flock shall be cut off from the fold, and there shall be no herd in the stalls: yet I will rejoice in the Lord, I will joy in the God of my salvation" (Hab. 3:17-18).

Looking beyond the storm brings comfort. A day is coming when evil and suffering will end. John describes that glorious day so beautifully: "And I saw a new heaven and the first earth was passed away; and there was no more sea. And I John saw the holy city, new Jerusalem, coming down from God out of heaven, prepared as a bride adorned for her husband. And I heard a great voice out of heaven saying, Behold, the tabernacle of God is with men, and he will dwell with them, and they shall be his people and God himself shall be with them, and be their God. And God shall wipe away all tears from their eyes; and there shall be no more death, neither sorrow, nor crying, neither shall there be any more pain; for the former things are passed away" (Rev. 21:1-4).

Yes, there are three ways to look at our storms. Looking *at* the storm only brings confusion. Looking *through* the storm brings confidence. Looking *beyond* the storm brings comfort.

When the storms come (and they most surely will) do not just look at the storm, but look through the storm and beyond the storm to trace your rainbow in the rain. Then you can sing with George Matheson:

> O love that will not let me go
> I rest my weary soul in Thee;
> I give Thee back the life I owe
> That in thine ocean depths its flow
> May richer, fuller be.
>
> O joy that seekest me through pain
> I cannot close my heart to thee;
> I TRACE THE RAINBOW THROUGH THE RAIN,
> And feel the promise is not vain
> That morn shall tearless be.

2
Tracing the Rainbow Through the Rain: Adverse Circumstances

Adverse Circumstances

Revelation 1:9-10

9 I John, who also am your brother, and companion in tribulation, and in the kingdom and patience of Jesus Christ, was in the isle that is called Patmos, for the word of God, and for the testimony of Jesus Christ. 10 I was in the Spirit on the Lord's day, and heard behind me a great voice, as of a trumpet.

John had his Isle of Patmos. Paul had his Mamertine Prison. John Milton had his blindness. Another John, Bunyan, had his Bedford Jail for twelve years. Commander Ralph Gaither, author of *With God in a POW Camp*, had the notorious "Hanoi Hilton" for seven years and eight months of North Vietnamese abuse.

And you have had your handicaps, your jails—real or imagined—your infirmities, your adversities. None of them are appealing and pleasant.

All of us who studied high school English lit were exposed to Longfellow's "The Rainy Day" which closes with:

Be still, sad heart! and cease repining;
Behind the clouds is the sun still shining:
Thy fate is the common fate of all:
Into each life some rain must fall,
Some days must be dark and dreary.

39

But many of us have asked, "If it has to rain, why does it have to pour? Why does it have to storm?" Only if it rains can you trace the rainbow through the rain! Pardon my use of a cliché, but we can't have roses without the thorns! Yes, it often appears that troubles come in bunches, and we ask all kinds of penetrating questions of our preachers—most of all, we ask them of God.

Living in certain places and under particular circumstances is easy. Living in other places under other circumstances can be adverse—and at times even downright difficult and oppressive.

Not long ago our family enjoyed several days of vacation at Maggie Valley, North Carolina, a quaint little hamlet in the Smoky Mountains. For the Hawkins four it was like stepping into another world. The scenario is vastly different from the hectic metropolis of Fort Lauderdale. At Maggie Valley we could more easily concentrate on the twitter of birds, the scampering of the deer, the sigh of the breeze in the trees, and the babble of the brooks.

Fort Lauderdale is gorgeous, but it is also bustling and hustling. It is teeming with pedestrians and traffic; hurry and scurry are prevalent. In Maggie Valley the folks wave and smile to each other on the roads and the few streets. They still hang their wash out on the line in the backyard. Trout swim lazily through the mountain streams, and the deer seem to run in slow motion along the mountainsides.

In that little village the townspeople's idea of a traffic jam is when two cars reach an intersection simultaneously. All around are dirt roads, cattle guards (they call 'em gaps), and picket fences. We ate several meals at Mrs. Sutton's Cafe. Sometimes we would be the only diners. That sweet mountain lady would emerge from the kitchen, sit down at our table, and visit with us. Over Mrs. Sutton's vegetable soup and apple pie we talked about what could solve all of the world's problems. Down in the valley was the little Baptist church pastored by the man whom God had called to that place in the mountains. On the Lord's Day the believers gather to worship there and to enjoy all of the pleasantries of their mountain home.

On Saturday we flew back to Fort Lauderdale and to our own reality. Carrying our luggage out of the airport we were confronted by taxi drivers cursing and fighting over fares. Climbing into our taxicab, our eyes, ears, and noses were accosted as our driver headed down Federal Highway, warding off the irritable and thoughtless drivers who, in bumper-to-bumper traffic, continued to keep their horns honking.

Sitting beside our two precious girls, we had not gone two blocks until we passed the local prostitutes standing on street corners in their bikinis and high heels, waving people over to the sidewalk. Row after row of adult movie houses and porno shops assaulted our eyes. Blatant pictures of unclad women were in the front windows.

A few blocks down the street we passed adult motels with suggestive slogans on their marquees, advertising waterbeds and mirrored ceilings. The driver then turned onto Broward Boulevard, and we saw so many of the people who sleep nightly on the streets of our city. The cab then drove west toward our home, passing by still more topless-bottomless night clubs and homosexual bars.

After unpacking and climbing into bed, I opened the evening paper to read of multiple murders and robberies that are daily occurrences in our part of the world. To be quite honest, all that kept me on Broward Boulevard that evening was the calling of God to our city.

Why is it so oppressive in certain places? I returned home to an area of illicit sex, drugs, murders, and secret sins that Mrs. Sutton and the other inhabitants of Maggie Valley seldom, if ever, talk about.

Then I began to mull over the servants of God who serve in forbidding and unsavory circumstances. Southern Baptist missionary William Wallace lost his life in a Chinese Communist prison. Mother Teresa is known for her ministry to lepers. Jonah was compelled to make the trip to Ninevah. Too long Abraham and his nephew, "just" Lot, lived in the environs of Sodom and Gomorrah. Paul influenced the vast Roman Empire from a jail cell, or either from a house which he had to rent. My mind rolled on, and then I came to a resounding conclusion: *It's not where we are. It's what we are!* And my heart sang amid my chagrin, disgust, and pain over the hellish sins of our city and countless cities around the world.

The aged apostle John expressed it in these words. "I John . . . was in the isle that is called Patmos . . . I was in the Spirit on the Lord's Day." John originally did not want to be there. The fact is: the old preacher was exiled there by the government. Even though he had freedom within certain limitations, he was removed from his mainland brothers and sisters in Christ.

When dealing with unsavory circumstances, many want to run away, to pull up stakes. Of course, John couldn't do that. He was there, and the Lord God made the most of John's circumstances. According to some conservative scholars, John wrote not only the Revelation while he was exiled to Patmos but perhaps one of his other Books as well. Isn't that amazing?

Servant of the Lord, right now you may be smarting under your circumstances. Day by day you ask yourself and God, "Why do I have to stay here? Why can't I find another place?" Maybe you are crying for a new business position, but you are rooted. You have filled out a hundred resumés for work with other firms, but nothing happens. Most of the companies do not even dignify your application by writing you a letter of rejection.

And Brother Pastor, you have stormed the gates of heaven praying for another church, another town or city, another opportunity—a fresh start. And even if the committees comes to hear you, they may turn away. They may or may not talk with you, but maybe you have that sinking feeling as the committee piles into their car(s) or van and drives off into the distance.

It's not easy to stay put. Many pastors, seemingly unappreciated and often disappointed, toy with the alien idea of "leaving the ministry." So many of them could salvage their ministries if they would latch onto the resources of God available through prayer and the Holy Spirit. Dear brother, maybe God wants you to hang in there and "trace the rainbow through the rain" as the Lord stands with you in those heartbreaking moments of despondency. I still believe if God brought you to that place of service, He is resourceful enough to open a place for you when His time comes.

Paul had his "thorn in the flesh," and we are going to have ours. Adverse circumstances and situations are incredible places to count for the Lord Jesus.

James Chalmers, the incomparable Scottish missionary to the headhunters of New Guinea, testified while on furlough in Scotland:

> I have had twenty-one years' experience among the South Sea Islanders, and for at least nine years of my life I have lived with the savages of New Guinea. I have seen the semicivilized and the uncivilized. I have lived with the Christian native, and I have lived, dined, and slept with the cannibal. But I have not yet met a single man or woman, or a single people, that your civilization without Christianity has civilized. Wherever there has been the slightest spark of civilized life in the Southern Seas, it has been because the gospel has been preached there; and wherever you find in the island of New Guinea a friendly people that will welcome you, there the missionaries of the cross have been preaching Christ.

It's not where you are—it's what you are that really matters. Even though you may be on your personal Patmos, you can be in the Spirit on the Lord's Day.

And I continued thinking and musing: *if I think Fort Lauderdale can be adverse, what about Patmos?* Patmos is a barren, rugged chunk of land to this day. Ten miles long and six miles wide, it is located a few miles off the Asia Minor coast of the Mediterranean. It is desolate, uninhabited, and mountainous. You could call it a Mediterranean Alcatraz.

The Romans used it as sort of a penal colony—a place to exile hard-core convicts, revolutionaries, mental cases, and the elderly. It had become a zoo housing many wild human beings.

The Caesar considered himself a god, constructing statues of himself and having them placed in worship areas throughout the Empire. By imperial edict the people were supposed to worship the images or statues and cry out loud, "Caesar is lord." If people refused, they met a terrible fate. Polycarp, the pastor of the church at Smyrna, was burned at the stake. Ignatius, the pastor at Antioch, was torn apart by wild beasts. With the exception of devout Christians, the majority of Roman subjects bowed down and worshiped Caesar. Innumerable followers of the Christ were brutally tortured and murdered merely because they would not repeat the phrase, "Caesar is lord." Their rebuttal was "Jesus Christ is Lord."

John, often called "The Beloved," was the brother of James. They were the sons of Zebedee (see Matt. 4:21-22; Mark 1:19-20). It is interesting that Jesus nicknamed James and John "Boanerges," meaning "the sons of thunder." "Thunder" could have referred to their father, Zebedee, who might have had a violent, explosive temper. Or the term might have indicated that James and John themselves, like their friend Simon Peter, were given to outbursts of temper and roughness.

Regardless of the meaning, John became the premier proponent of love. In his own Gospel, John refers to himself as "one of His disciples, whom Jesus loved" (see John 13:23). At the Last Supper, Peter had especially become paranoid when the Master prophesied, "Verily, verily, I say unto you, that one of you shall betray me" (John 13:21).

The disciples began looking at one another at a loss to know of which one He was speaking. There was reclining on Jesus' breast one of His disciples, whom Jesus loved. Simon Peter therefore gestured to him, and said to him, "Tell us who it is of whom He is speaking." He, leaning back thus on Jesus' breast, said to Him, "Lord, who is it?" (John 13:22-25, NASB).

John actually asked the question for Peter.

According to the biblical account, John was the only apostle who stuck with Jesus until the end.

Now there stood by the cross of Jesus his mother, and his mother's sister, Mary the wife of Cleophas, and Mary Magdalene. When Jesus therefore saw his mother, and the disciple standing by, whom he loved, he saith unto his mother, Woman, behold thy son! Then saith he to the disciple, Behold thy mother! And from that hour that disciple took her unto his own home (John 19:25-27).

Jesus left his dear mother under the watchcare of none other than John. No wonder John felt an extraordinary bond of love with the Savior and delighted in calling himself the one "whom Jesus loved."

Christian tradition has it that John cared for Mary, as he would his own mother, until her death. He was the bishop or pastor at Ephesus for many years. The people loved him and he loved them, all because of the Lord Jesus' *agape* love.

Many think that John was finally released from Patmos when he was almost 100 years old and that he returned to Ephesus. He was so feeble that men would carry him into the services, and he would repeat again and again, "Little children, love one another, love one another!"

As he was moved by the Holy Spirit to write the Revelation, there he was—banished to a barren rock island to live out his "golden years" among the criminals and insane on Patmos. Why was John there at the age of ninety or more? The answer is obvious: "because of the word of God and the testimony of Jesus Christ."

He had refused to compromise. Read our text once again: "I John, who also am your brother and companion in tribulation, and in the kingdom and patience of Jesus Christ, was in the isle that is called Patmos, for the word of God, and for the testimony of Jesus Christ. I was in the Spirit on the Lord's day, and heard behind me a great voice, as of a trumpet." Through the Spirit, John knew that it's not where you are—it's what you are that counts.

Right now many of us are experiencing our own personal Patmoses. Years ago there was a Spike Jones ditty that ended "I'm feeling mighty low." That's how many of us feel in our exile. We pray for relief from these adverse circumstances. At times we are caught in situations totally beyond our control. True, sometimes we erect our own Patmoses, our own Alcatrazes—sometimes. If only we could remember that John was on—of all places—Patmos, but he was "in the Spirit." That makes the difference, for the sense of God's presence can transform Patmos into paradise.

On Patmos we view:

Liabilities

People might well ask, "What could a ninety-year-old man accomplish isolated on a desolate rock, away from friends and kinfolks, and in a state of veritable solitary confinement?" A good answer: commune personally with the Lord Jesus Christ and write at least one book of the New Testament! Oh ... John could have worried about his liabilities, his handicaps. There was no office of Social Security and old-age assistance. There is no mention of how he lived—what he wore, what he ate, what he drank, what he transcribed this marvelous message on. He was there, all the better to receive revelation from the King of kings and Lord of lords.

His surroundings were adverse; his situation was adverse; his setup was adverse. Surrounding Patmos was the vast sea. "Water, water everywhere." It reminds you of those lines from "The Ancient Mariner." Perhaps he had no particular place to sleep, like his Lord who testified that foxes had holes and the birds of the air had nests, but that the Son of man had no place to lay His head. Maybe John had to scrounge for food. You can be sure that he didn't have fare fit for the emperor. Our personal Patmoses also seem full of liabilities. The adverse seas beat and surge.

The tragedy is: Some have eyes only for Patmos. Amid bad situations, it is easy to fall into the trap of "I-was-on-the-isle-of-Patmos Syndrome," and see only liabilities.

But wait a minute. That's one side of the story. Yes, he was on Patmos, but he was *in the Spirit*. Notice how many biblical heroes were in prison at one time or another. If they were living today, they would be considered jailbirds. In the eyes of the world, they would have "criminal records." Joseph, Daniel, Shadrach, Meshach, and Abednego, Jeremiah, John the Baptist, Peter, this very John, Paul, Silas, Stephen (before the Sanhedrin), James the brother of Jesus, and many more.

Through Christ the liabilities were turned into Lordship. John reveled in the purpose of God, in the Lordship of Christ, in the sovereignty of God. God was in control. God neither slumbered nor slept but kept watch over him. God is a very present help in the time of trouble. At least sixty years before, Jesus had spoken these prophetic words to his followers, and John was among them:

10 Blessed are they which are persecuted for righteousness' sake; for theirs is the kingdom of heaven. 11 Blessed are ye, when men shall revile you, and persecute you, and shall say all manner of evil against you falsely, for my sake. 12 Rejoice and be exceeding glad: for great is your reward in heaven: for so persecuted they the prophets which were before you (Matt. 5:10-12).

John was also there when Jesus foretold: "Then shall they deliver you up to be afflicted, and shall kill you: and ye shall be hated of all nations for my name's sake" (Matt. 24:9). On another occasion he had heard these words escape Jesus' lips: "These things I have spoken unto you, that in me ye might have peace. In the world ye shall have tribulation: but be of good cheer; I have overcome the world" (John 16:33). John was intent on his purpose for being on Patmos, and the purpose unfolded in the writing of this apocalypse. God opened up heaven, giving John a revelation to share with all posterity.

"I was on the isle of Patmos . . . and I was in the Spirit." Some think of Patmos, while others think of the Spirit. It is attitude, not atmosphere, that really matters. Many a spiritual giant has risen from the ghettos, the slums, and abject poverty. Those people focused on the Spirit rather than adverse circumstances. They fought the rats and roaches as best they could, but they did not use their adverse circumstances as an alibi for defeatism and failure.

Many a person behind jail bars has testified, "God put me here behind these walls so I could hear the gospel and be saved." If the late and great Billy Sunday had not gone slumming one night in Chicago, he might not have dropped into the Pacific Garden Mission, where he was saved. Listen to me. Look past the liabilities to the Lord. O. S. Hawkins is privileged to be in Fort Lauderdale. It is God's spot for me. Did it ever occur to you that your adverse circumstances might be God's will for you? Perhaps this is what moved the songwriter to ask:

Am I a soldier of the cross, a follower of the lamb?
And shall I fear to own His cause, or blush to speak His name?
Must I be carried to the skies on flow'ry beds of ease
While others fought to win the prize, and sailed through bloody seas?
Are there no foes for me to face? Must I not stem the flood?
Is this vile world a friend to grace, to help me on to God?

> Sure I would fight if I would reign; increase my courage, Lord
> I'll bear the toil, endure the pain, supported by Thy Word.

The true followers of the Lamb will trace the rainbow through the rain of liabilities. Your liabilities can be lost in Lordship. You do not need to bemoan your liabilities. Leave them at the pierced feet of our triumphant Lord. On Patmos there are also

Limitations

Talk about limitations! Patmos was overstocked with them. For many of us, looking at the Mediterranean would be a delight, especially if we could choose our land mass—maybe the French Riviera, the Isle of Capri, or another exotic spot. Looking at the expanse of the Mediterranean would be marvelous for a while, but suppose you were living on a rock and had to look at it endlessly? Every morning John awoke, and there was the sea, and it was not like the glassy sea in heaven. Unless the government provided lodging for him (and there is no indication it did), at night he had to search for a place to lay his tired, old head. Many nights he looked out at the moonlight reflected across that sea.

He was cut off, isolated. Out of control. He could not visit his friends; he could not attend his church; he could not take a leisurely stroll through the marketplace. He was limited in his resources for study. His parchments and books were far away in Ephesus or destroyed by now. More than likely he seldom ever heard from home.

Are you living on Patmos? Do you feel limited? Isolated and cut off? I beg of you not to fall into a Patmos fixation. God is on the throne, even on your Patmos. With all of the limitations, it is easy for us to forget that Jesus is Lord. In your liabilities and limitations, God can perform His mighty miracles through you. Yes, *you!*

I fully believe that when John spoke the words, "I was in the Spirit," the limitations gave way to liberty. In the truest sense, he was no longer a prisoner. He was free! Madame Guyon, whose

Spirit-filled writings still bless untold thousands—perhaps even millions—wrote "A Prisoner's Song" while in the notorious Bastille during the French Revolution. The fourth and fifth stanzas express the thought of liabilities giving way to liberty:

> My cage confines me round;
>   Abroad I cannot fly;
> But though my wing is closely bound,
>   My heart's at liberty;
> My prison walls cannot control
> The flight, the freedom of my soul.
>
> Oh, it is good to soar
>   These bolts and bars above,
> To Him whose purpose I adore,
>   Whose providence I love;
> And in thy mighty will to find
> The joy, the freedom of the mind.

John was not really a prisoner. He was free. His predecessor at the Ephesian church was the apostle Paul. Paul was imprisoned in Rome as he wrote the Prison Epistles—Philippians, Colossians, and Philemon. It is thought he was chained to a guard twenty-four hours a day. Still, he was free in the Spirit. Earlier he had written the Galatians this message: "Stand fast in the liberty wherewith Christ hath set you free, and be not entangled again with the yoke of bondage" (5:1). John had the deep realization that there is liberty wherever the Spirit of the Lord is.

While on Patmos, the majority looks at the liabilities. The faith-filled, daring few look at liberty.

Finally, on Patmos we see

Loneliness

There is no proof of the claim that loneliness is the number-one cause of suicide. Many think it is. It is almost redundant for me to state that Patmos was lonely, but it was. John probably had few companions. He was surrounded by human jackals, hard-hearted men who probably left John to himself. John must have longed for his family and friends and for his brothers and sisters in the church at Ephesus. When the Lord's day rolled around, he must have longed to fellowship with the saints and to deliver God's Word to them.

Pastor friend. Yes, you on Patmos. Sometimes do you remember that sweet, little church of days gone by? When the Lord's day comes, do you smell that fresh country air? Do you hear the old untrained song leader making a joyful noise? Do you hear Miss Clara or Miss Minnie playing at the ancient upright? Amid all the programming, all of the committee meetings, all the hubbub of your present situation, do you ever yearn for that little country church tucked in the hollow. I imagine you do.

And bless your heart, preacher without a church. When God called you, he meant you to do exactly your calling—preaching the glorious Word of God. And you will never be happy until you are doing it. Even if a church does not open up, there are clinics, old folks homes, jails, prisons, and reform schools. If you are called, God will give you a place to preach. In fact, He will help you make a place!

Sometime ago a man was saved in our services. In conversation with him afterwards, he explained how he previously frequented bars every night of the week. Since he had mentioned that he didn't drink, I asked him why he would spend his time in bars. He replied, "I was so lonely I just wanted to hear other people's voices. I used to go and sit in night clubs just to listen to other people talk to each other." People all around us are living on that kind of Patmos.

Some have eyes only for Patmos. They never look beyond the rocks and the sea. Their eyes are riveted on their problems and not their possibilities. Loneliness looms large. But John's loneliness gave way to love. He was in the Spirit on the Lord's day.

Paul had written: "And now abideth faith, hope, and love, these three but the greatest of these is charity [love]." In his letter to the Romans, he had asked the rhetorical question: "Who shall separate us from the love of Christ? Shall tribulation, or distress, or persecution, of famine, or nakedness, or peril, or sword? As it is written, For thy sake we are killed all the day long; we are accounted as sheep for the slaughter. Nay, in all these things we are more than conquerors through him that loved us. For I am persuaded, that neither death, nor life, nor angels, nor principalities, nor powers, nor things present, nor things to come, Nor height, nor depth, nor any other creature shall be able to separate us from the love of God, which is in Christ Jesus our Lord" (Rom. 8:35-39).

The love of Christ was with John on the isle, and loneliness had stepped aside for the indwelling love of God. Love is the key. "God commended [demonstrated] his love toward us, in that, while we were yet sinners, Christ died for us" (Rom. 5:8). Leave your loneliness for the love of God.

John learned the truth. You are learning it, I hope. I am moving in that direction. It's not *where* you are that matters the most. It's *who* you are that matters. You are a follower of the Lord Jesus. You have His liberty, His lordship, His love. To be quite honest, I'm a long distance from the Maggie Valleys of this world, but I'm honored that the Master has counted me worthy to serve here in Fort Lauderdale.

So, many discover themselves on an island of liabilities, limitations, and loneliness, but that personal Patmos, when turned over to the Spirit of God, can be lost in lordship, liberty, and love. Sometimes it seems that Patmos will do us in. Liabilities, limitations, and loneliness are doing their dastardly work.

But wait. What about asking God to let you be in the Spirit on the Lord's day?

When we are in the Spirit, God assumes His Lordship and gives us meaning and purpose for life. He presents us liberty and sets the captive free. He envelops us in *agape* love, unconditional love.

Hear me. Are you in the Spirit? It's not where we are that matters. It's what we are. And that truth helps us to trace the rainbow through the rain!

3
Tracing the Rainbow Through the Rain: Loneliness

Loneliness

Genesis 28:10-16

10 Then Jacob departed from Beersheba and went toward
Haran. 11 And he came to a certain place and spent the night,
because the sun had set; and he took one of the stones of the
place and put it under his head, and lay down in that place. 12
And he had a dream, and behold, a ladder was set on the earth
with its top reaching to heaven; and behold, the angels of God
were ascending and descending on it. 13 And behold, the Lord
stood above it and said, "I am the Lord, the God of your father
Abraham and the God of Isaac; the land on which you lie, I will
give it to you and to your descendants. 14 Your descendants shall
also be like the dust of the earth, and you shall spread out to the
west and to the east and to the north and to the south; and in you
and your descendants shall all the families of the earth be
blessed. 15 And behold, I am with you, and will keep you
wherever you go, and I will bring you back to this land; for I will
not leave you until I have done what I have promised you." 16
Then Jacob awoke from his sleep and said, "Surely the Lord is
in this place, and I did not know it" (NASB).

Students of human behavior have observed that loneliness is
the number-one plague facing Americans. Is that not also true of
mankind at large? "The pain of loneliness is universal," wrote Ida
Nelle Hollaway.[1]

Thomas Wolfe, the famous novelist, penned these lines:

> Loneliness, far from being a rare and curious phenomenons . . .
> is the central and inevitable fact of human existence. When we
> examine the moments, acts and statements of all kinds of peo-
> ple—not only the grief and ecstasy of the greatest poets, but also
> the huge unhappiness of the average soul, as evidenced by the
> innumerable strident words of abuse, hatred, contempt, mistrust
> and scorn that forever grate upon our ears as the manswarm
> passes us in the streets—we find, I think, that they are all suffer-
> ing from the same thing. The final cause of their complaint is
> loneliness.[2]

A sense of loneliness has permeated literature, music, and
drama. Through the years, songs of loneliness have flowed over the
airwaves—"None but the Lonely Heart," "Alone Again Naturally," "One Alone," "All by Myself," Bluer than Blue, Sadder
Than Sad," "Feelings," "You're Only Lonely," "Only the
Lonely," and even "You Picked a Fine Time to Leave Me, Lucille."
I could fill up this chapter with song titles. Ditto with books about
loneliness, depression, sorrow, and forsakenness. Motion pictures
and plays are shot through with loneliness. Carson McCullers,
who is also well-remembered for *A Member of the Wedding,* wrote
The Heart Is a Lonely Hunter. Arthur Miller's *Death of a Salesman*
is indeed a tragedy of isolation and loneliness.

Therefore, we should not feel surprised that loneliness appears
early in the Word of God. It was God the Creator who decided "It
is not good for the man to be alone" (Gen. 2:18*a*, NASB). And
there are theologians who claim that God created mankind because
He, the Creator God of the universe, was lonely and wanted fellowship and companionship with His creatures.

Young Jacob was haunted by this same feeling of being cut off,
estranged, isolated, barren, and alone. In Genesis 28 he was exist-
ing in a state of loneliness for this was his first time away from

home. Jacob's hunter-brother, Esau, was used to the vast outdoors. But that was not the case with Jacob, the "homebody," the cook and errand boy for his mother, Rebekah. He was accustomed to being by the home fires and enjoyed the sound of human voices and the comforts of home.

Now he was alone and grappling with a gnawing sense of loneliness, accompanied by fear of the unknown and fear for his life itself. It reminds you of a song by Merle Haggard—"This Loneliness Is Eating Me Alive." And loneliness was doing exactly that to Jacob.

Then the sun began to descend below the horizon. In spite of the Oriental heat, it soon began to chill. The fingers of darkness crept over the land. It always seems to become lonelier when that happens. Fearful, nervous Jacob began to seek a place to rest. He thought of his warm pallet back home and the solicitous voice of his mother. Perhaps he longed for her good-night kisses.

There were no pillow, no furnishings for a bed, so he substituted a rock and lay down fitfully. No doubt his fevered brain returned to family laughter of bygone days. But then each noise of nighttime stirred up uneasiness and fright within Jacob. Every rustling leaf, every nocturnal insect, every slight breeze, every call of a night animal or bird conjured up visions of harm and calamity.

Young Jacob finally dozed off to sleep and God visited him. In a dream God presented a vision of a ladder which reached clear to the throne of heaven. There was young Jacob, fearful and frightened, with a stone pillow and nothing for cover but the black blanket of night. The Almighty never cares about our surroundings when He chooses to visit us.

Maybe you can identify with Jacob—living in loneliness.

Lonely people include the executive on the way up who no longer talks to his wife; the young man or woman alone for the first time in an apartment complex in a large city; the suburban housewife surrounded by small children and by neighbors whom she does not know. There are lonely people among the "swingers" who spend their evenings in darkened bars, hoping for someone to talk with. Couples who have just moved for the third time in two years may be lonely. They despair of making friends before they have to take up roots again because of a job transfer. The airlines personnel who meet many people on airplanes, know very few. The salesman who has to travel all week, and his wife who stays home alone, may both be lonely. Don't forget the "migratory workers," a group which includes more people than just those who follow the crops. Professional sportsmen, entertainers, long-distance truck drivers, oil specialists, and scientific engineers, as well as military personnel, are all "migratory workers." They have to travel long distances in order to do their work.[3]

We live in the midst of loneliness, and all of us have lonely periods. A husband and wife have an argument. They are momentarily estranged emotionally. She retreats to the bedroom and closes the door. He buries himself in a football game on TV or drives off to play video games. Even though they may love each other dearly, they are temporarily lonely in spirit. No person is free of feeling lonely, even amid a crowd of people.

Walk down a busy street and intently watch faces. You will come away downtrodden, noticing pain, sadness, upset, and sometimes blank, stoic stares. At least half of the people will be single—never-married, widowed, or divorced. Divorce is of epidemic proportions, and many people are merely living together—thus, when a living-together couple breaks up, there is no statistic on the books, but deep emotional and psychic pain is nearly always the result.

And many people are not gregarious and outgoing. They have difficulty relating and making friends; they tend to become more and more withdrawn into themselves, and they often feel that no one cares.

In this chapter I present four secrets that will enable us not only to deal with loneliness, but to overcome it—and to live beyond it. Part of our problem is that we all too often deal with the fruits and not the roots. Until we begin to deal with the root, we will simply continue on a never-ending treadmill of loneliness, never actually moving but staying in the same spot, even though we are desperately trying to make progress.

As we focus on Jacob for an example, let us examine some reasons, a remedy, a revelation, and a response to loneliness.

Reasons

10 And Jacob went out from Beersheba, and went toward Haran.
11 And he lighted upon a certain place and tarried there all night because the sun was set; and he took of the stones of that place, and put them for his pillows, and lay down in that place to sleep (KJV).

Why does loneliness set in? Before continuing, let us not confuse two words—alone and lonely. They are not necessarily synonymous. I know many people who are alone but not lonely. I know of others who are surrounded by people, and yet they live in loneliness. What makes the difference? We are coming to the answer momentarily.

Why was Jacob lonely? One solid reason is: he was lonely because his betrayed, double-crossed, irate brother, Esau, was in hot pursuit of Jacob. Every Sunday School child has heard the story of how Jacob, egged on by his mother, connived to steal the birthright which, by Hebrew custom and tradition, belonged to Esau. No wonder Jacob's name meant "trickster" or "supplanter." Why was Jacob lonely? Most would reply that Jacob was lonely because his brother was chasing him, and they would stop right there—no analysis, no going deeper.

Yet, we ought to proceed one step farther. Why was Esau chasing him? The answer is self-evident. Jacob had cheated, lied, stolen, and done treacherously. Jacob never learned to handle his isolation and loneliness until he began to assume responsibility for his deeds.

Society is filled with people sometimes called sociopaths and, in extreme cases, psychopaths. They never accept the blame, even if they are wrong a thousand times. They despise responsibility. They are never to blame; others are always at fault. Over a period of time, these people build up far-out defense mechanisms for themselves and become totally blinded concerning their own condition.

All of us have a streak of sociopathy. All of us have sinned and come short of the glory of God. "All we like sheep have gone astray." Our hearts are deceitful above all things and are desperately wicked. As my friend Grady Wilson put it, "There's a little bit of Watergate in all of us." It is easy to blame our "Esaus" for the predicaments in which we find ourselves, all too often self-induced difficulties. The habit of "passing the buck" started in the Garden of Eden. Adam blamed Eve, and Eve blamed the serpent. But Adam and Eve did it, not the serpent. He merely laid the temptation in front of them. Eve could have refused the fruit. So could have Adam. Years ago there was a song, "Put the Blame on Mame, Boys." Put the blame on Esau, put the blame on the devil—but never yourself. And that's why people can never overcome estrangement and loneliness. They never seem to realize that they might sometimes have a hand in their own loneliness.

Quite frankly, many are lonely because of sinful and unscrupulous schemes and actions like Jacob. Others are lonely because of present failures. Still others are lonely because of future bugaboos. Loneliness is often associated with ingrown self-pity.

Once a young man visited the study of the late and great preacher, T. Dewitt Talmage. He lamented, "Dr. Talmage, I have no will to live. I'm not sure of my salvation. In fact, I'm not even sure about the existence of God. I really wish I were dead!" Dr.

Talmage replied, after the young man had requested the church to remove him from the roll, "All right, we will remove you if that is your wish, but first I want to send you out on an assignment. Will you go?" The fellow would and did.

Dr. Talmage asked the young man to visit an old man who was dying of cancer. Reluctantly, the fellow left to contact the man, who lived in a decaying section of the city.

Hours later the fellow returned and happened to catch Dr. Talmage in his office. With a radiant light on his face, the young man exulted, "Dr. Talmage, it was wonderful. I visited the old man in his rags and poverty. Would you believe it?—the man asked me how he could be saved and could prepare to meet his God. As best I could I showed him the plan of salvation. He bowed his head, Dr. Talmage, and called on the Lord to save him! His last words to me were, 'Son, you are an angel. I'm ready to meet God now. Thank you so much for coming!' Dr. Talmage, leave my name on the roll, and give me another assignment for visitation!"

In a short time the young man had his relationship with the Lord rekindled. He had discovered a secret: Only by staying busy for God can we overcome depression, doubt, and self-pity.

Jacob was responsible for his own loneliness. The primary reason for Jacob's loneliness, and ours, is that we shut ourselves in and others out. The poet Edwin Markham fashioned these immortal lines:

> He drew a circle that shut me out—
> Heretic, rebel, a think to flout.
> But Love and I had the wit to win:
> We drew a circle that took him in!

The morbidly lonely person is often avoided by others. They recoil from negativism and self-pity. "Misery loves company," the old expression goes, and people want no part of miserable self-pity. People cannot stand self-pity. Write it down and underline it in red:

Loneliness is not so much a matter of isolation as it is of insulation. I have no idea how you actually feel—I cannot plumb the depths of your heart. Only the All-seeing Eye can. Perhaps I would react exactly as you do to your own particular set of circumstances. But I remind you that insulation is not the way out of your dilemma. If we are ever to wrestle with and win over loneliness, we must dig down to the root cause. Most of the time we find ourselves there.

Amazingly, many attractive, vivacious people become lonely derelicts. Are you lonely? At the same time, are you willing to touch the sensitive nerve? Are you willing to do a "root canal" of your inner being? Do not shrug off the causes of your loneliness. Begin by asking, "What do I have to do with it? Are only others to blame? Why am I in this fix?"

There is a possibility that your loneliness is the result of circumstances beyond your control, but that possibility is rare. The biblical principal goes: "Be not deceived; God is not mocked: for whatsoever a man soweth, that shall he also reap" (Gal. 6:7). The simple truth is: We will reap what we sow. It applies in all of life. One preacher called it "The Law of the Harvest."

The fact is: If we are lonely, we should find another lonely person and pour our lives into them. If we merely open ourselves, before long people will materialize from all over, ministering life and love to us. Many of us are "Dead Sea" Christians. The Dead Sea receives, and the flow stops there. Bodies of water can stagnate unless there is a flowing in and flowing out. Many people are on the receiving end too much of the time. Believe it or not, the more you receive without giving, the deeper you will sink into isolation, insulation, and loneliness.

This is a prevalent sin among church members. Many of them join the church and think in terms of "what has the church done for me?" Somehow they never seem to understand that when a person embraces Jesus Christ, the tables are turned. In Christ, even for the brand-new Christian, there is supposed to be service toward others. Life in Christ is a radical move away from preoccupation with self—self-obsession, self-worship, self-pity. Christianity is a gospel of giving.

Paul on the road to Damascus first asked, "Who art thou, Lord?" Perhaps he already knew, but it is clear that when Jesus' identity was established in Paul's mind, he immediately asked, "Lord, what wilt thou have me to do?" That's one of the first questions a born-again believer ought to ask.

Too many of us have been building walls instead of bridges. Loneliness will abate as we, through Christ's name, reach out to others.

Then I want you to notice a . . .

Remedy

> 12 And he dreamed, and behold a ladder set up on the earth, and the top of it reached to heaven: and behold the angels of God ascending and descending on it. 13 And behold, the Lord stood above it, and said, I am the Lord God of Abraham thy father; and the God of Isaac: the land whereon thou liest to thee will I give it, and to thy seed: 14 And thy seed shall be as the dust of the earth, and thou shalt spread abroad to the west, and to the east, and to the north, and to the south; and in thee and in thy seed shall all the families of the earth be blessed (KJV).

After Jacob had fallen asleep, the Lord showed him the remedy for loneliness. How? Jacob became aware of the Lord's abiding presence. Thankfully, many of us have had special experiences with the Lord in the nick of time . . . just when we needed them most. Maybe it was a verse or passage of Scripture which became your *rhema,* your special word for that occasion. Perhaps it was a sermon, and you felt every word was prepared especially for you in your condition. Or it was a clear-cut answer to prayer . . . or deliverance from the jaws of death . . . or a person who entered your life (and later you asked yourself, *Was that God's angel sent to me?*).

In a moment of your loneliness—as you traced the rainbow through the rain—God has revealed Himself to you. For that time you felt that no one on the face of the earth ever had exactly that kind of close, intimate relationship with the Lord. Yes, you felt *special* to the Lord, and you are special to Him.

Jacob clung to the presence of God at Bethel. The prevailing presence of God was the remedy for his gnawing loneliness.

To me the ladder represents communion with God. I think in terms of the Lord Jesus being that ladder from earth to heaven. How I love that old chorus, "We Are Climbing Jacob's Ladder." The predominant truth is: God always takes the initiative with us. Christianity is not man seeking God—it is God seeking man. The entire meaning of God's Word is the seeking God who goes after his lost creatures. Christmas and Easter and every Christian observance point to the God who always takes the initiative.

The grace of God is manifestly revealed here in this passage. Jacob was a conniving, scheming fugitive who had lied and cheated. What had he done to deserve this holy moment with God? Nothing! He deserved exactly the opposite. And none of us have done anything to deserve the "marvelous grace of our loving Lord." Jesus, Himself the Ladder, stated in John 1:51: "Verily, verily, I say unto you, hereafter you shall see heaven open and the angels of God descending and ascending upon the Son of man." Jesus has reached down to where we are.

As Julia H. Johnston has expressed it:

> Marvelous grace of our loving Lord,
> Grace that exceeds our sin and our guilt,
> Yonder on Calvary's mount outpoured,
> There where the blood of the Lamb was spilt.

. . . .

> Marvelous, infinite, matchless grace,
> Freely bestowed on all who believe;

All who are longing to see His face,
Will you this moment His grace receive?

Grace, grace, God's grace,
Grace that will pardon and cleanse within;
Grace, grace, God's grace,
Grace that is greater than all our sin.

And none of us deserve this marvelous, infinite, matchless grace!

The Ladder is reaching down to you at this moment. He is the remedy. The ladder extended clear down to where Jacob lay in his lying, cheating, and stealing. Maybe you are presently lying in corruption and sin. Perhaps you consider yourself too sophisticated to admit your guilt, even to God who will listen to your confession in secret. Jesus, with every drop of His blood, reaches down to you.

Could it be that the bonds of sin are strangling the life out of you? Jesus will break those bonds and allow you to breath the invigorating breezes of heaven. You are lonely—then let Jesus fill the void within your heart and life. The weakest, vilest sinner can, through the Ladder of the Lord, climb from the pit of degredation to the foot of the eternal throne, and that is why we can sing.

Oh, the love that drew salvation's plan!
Oh, the grace that brought it down to man!
Oh, the mighty gulf that God did span
At Calvary!

—William R. Newell

Then we notice the angels. They ascended on the ladder, symbolic of our prayers going up to God, I believe. They descended, representative of our answers to those petitions. For years, many evangelicals shied away from the doctrine of angels. The Bible is chockfull of angels. I refer here to Hebrews 1:13-14: "But to which of the angels said he at any time, Sit on my right hand, until I make thine enemies thy footstool? Are they not all ministering spirits, sent forth to minister for them who shall be heirs of salvation?" In addition to the indwelling ministry of the Holy Spirit, the angels of God minister to us with comfort and with watchcare. What a sweeping relief when Jacob finally realized his reasons for loneliness and the remedy for it. We need never again yield to feelings of loneliness if we will remember that Jesus reaches down to where we are and loves us unconditionally.

Remember there is a difference between being alone and being lonely.

> Obviously, it is wrong to equate loneliness with being alone. Aloneness can be a blessing, a source of growth and of joy. On the other hand, being with others does not insulate us from loneliness. It is true to say that loneliness is a *feeling* of aloneness, a consciousness that no one can completely share our feelings or completely understand our thoughts.[4]

Being alone is an integral part of spiritual growth. How often we preachers have talked about "a quiet time" with God, and how few of us practice it! Our own Lord withdrew for fellowship with His Heavenly Father. Then He returned and ministered to the pressing, teeming throngs. It is abnormal not to seek solitude occasionally. One comedian feared being alone to the extent that he hired people to sit up with him all hours of the night. Sometimes he would finally fall asleep at four or five in the morning.

Many people hate solitude because they are afraid of introspection. They are afraid to face themselves in private! So they surround themselves with activity, hubbub, hustle. Those who habituate bars and taverns must receive extra power from the devil to drink glass after glass of booze and sit up all night, and then try to show up for work at 8 or 9 in the morning!

In being alone, Jacob met God. If he had surrounded himself with an entourage of laughing, talking companions, he never would've experienced this amazing encounter.

Has it occurred to you that more often than not God reveals His plan for our lives when we are alone? Moses was alone on the backside of the desert when God revealed Himself. Elijah was alone under a juniper tree when God came. And Jacob was alone with stones for a pillow when the Lord revealed Himself as the Ladder to heaven.

Being alone for a time is not all bad, then, is it? So you have plenty of time alone—by yourself? Have you ever thought of praising God for that time—those precious moments for communion with God, for collecting your wits, for going deeper in the Word, for writing a spiritual diary, and for generally growing as a follower of Christ Jesus? You can be alone, but you don't have to be lonely. There are reasons for loneliness, and there is a remedy for it. Then there is a

Revelation

15 And behold, I am with thee, and will keep thee in all places whither thou goest, and will bring thee again into this land; for I will not leave thee, until I have done that which I have spoken to thee of (KJV).

The "still small voice" can only be heard when all other voices have been hushed. What a magnificent revelation and promise God gave to Jacob that night! He received the promise of God's *divine presence.* Jacob felt lonely to the core, but the Lord assured Him, "I am with you."

If only we could realize that we are never truly alone when the Lord Jesus Christ lives within our hearts! B. B. McKinney wrote:

I've seen the lightning flashing,
I've heard the thunder roll.
I've seen storm's breakers dashing
Trying to conquer my soul.

I heard the voice of Jesus telling
Telling me still to fight on.
He promised never to leave me,
Never to leave me alone.

That was the promise of God to Jacob. I will never leave you alone. I will be with you. I will never forsake you. And many of us ought to hear that right now. In our loneliness we often feel that no one cares, that no one is there. But Jesus cares. And He is always there, but we have to be reminded of it.

Jacob also received the promise of God's *divine protection*. He had been cringing at the thought of Esau, but God declared, "I will keep you." You ought to hear that today. God has never gone back on His promises, not one time. He always follows through. When He promises to guide you, He will do it. When he promises His presence, He will be there. When He promises His protection, He will do precisely that—protect you. God continues to promise: "I will keep you in all the places you are going."

But there is even more. Jacob also received the promise of God's *divine preservation*. He felt forsaken by all his friends and most of his relations. He was bereft before God promised, "I will bring thee again into this land." Don't you need to hear that within your heart? At that moment you may see no escape out of your predicament. You may feel there is no way of coming back to the place you once were with God, but God promises that He will preserve you and restore you. Claim that promise as your own!

In these verses we also discover God's *divine promise*. God had emphatically promised Jacob He would carry on the seed of Abraham in the lineage of the coming Messiah, yet now the possibilities seemed remote . . . but God had promised, "I will not leave thee, until I have done that which I have spoken to thee of." Allow the Holy Spirit to fortify your heart with that truth. God is going to perform as He has promised. Lay aside your preoccupation with loneliness and forsakenness and trust God's absolute word.

These are comforting, precious words, but they belong only to those who camp at the foot of the cross which unites heaven and earth. Are you lonely? What are the reasons? Are you even partly responsible? There is a remedy for it. Jesus is reaching down to you right this moment, and the revelation is here. He will give you the promise of His presence and protection. Then will come your

Response

And Jacob awakened from his sleep, and he said, Surely the Lord is in this place, and I knew it not (v. 16).

What was Jacob's response when all of these factors began to mesh—when he began to realize the reasons for his loneliness, when he saw the Ladder reaching down as a remedy, and when he received the revelation of the promise of God's presence? He exclaimed, "Surely the Lord is in this place, and I knew it it not." God was there all the time, and I didn't even know it. Note the tenses—is and knew. And when all was said and done, God reaffirmed His promises: "I will not leave thee until I have accomplished my purpose," in essence.

Dear friend, in the words of Jacob, "Surely the Lord is in place, and I knew it not." He is in the place near you, and perhaps you are not aware of it. You who are lonely have the promise of God's Word. "The Lord is near to the broken-hearted,/And saves those who are crushed in spirit" (Ps. 34:18, NASB). Tender-hearted Jesus calls:

Come unto me, all ye that labour and are heavy laden, and I will give you rest. Take my yoke upon you, and learn of me; for I am meek and lowly in heart: and ye shall find rest unto your souls. For my yoke is easy, and my burden is light (Matt. 11:28-30).

Surely the Lord is in that place by you. The fact is, He has been there all the time. He was beside you in that bed of pain, and you might not have known it. He was with you in that precarious church, work, or home situation, and you knew it not. He walked with you on that rocky pathway, and you were not aware of it, even as the two disciples were unaware that Jesus was walking with them on the road to Emmaus. They were alongside Him but could not recognize that it was Jesus Himself.

He was weeping with you in your anguish and pain, and you knew it not. He was holding your hand in the deepest of despair, and you were insensitive. Yes, and He was there in those haunting moments of loneliness. Jesus was there all the time, and you might not have known it.

So, I challenge you to join Jacob in responding, "Surely the Lord was in this place, and I knew it not." It is intriguing to note in Genesis 28:19 that Jacob changed the name of the place from Luz to Bethel. Luz meant "separation," and that is what loneliness does. It separates us. But Bethel meant "house of God," the dwelling place of God Himself. To me, the change of names implies a spiritual lesson: we must separate ourselves from the world, and in so doing, we will enter the house of God.

As you step into the conscious presence of the Father, through the Ladder, you will declare: "Surely the Lord is in this place, and now I know it!" Glory in His presence. Praise Him for His providence. Thank Him for His protection. Magnify Him for His never-failing, never-ending promises.

Yet, some are seemingly locked into loneliness. Although no one else seems to understand, there is One who does. His name is Jesus. Annie B. Russell touchingly put it:

> There is never a day so dreary,
> There is never a night so long,
> But the soul that is trusting Jesus
> Will somewhere find a song.

. . . .

> There is never a care or burden,
> There is never a grief or loss,
> But that Jesus in love will lighten
> When carried to the cross.

> . . . .

> Wonderful, wonderful Jesus,
> In the heart He implanteth a song:
> A song of deliverance, of courage,
>   of strength,
> In the heart He implanteth a song.

"Wonderful, wonderful Jesus!" "His name is wonderful!" "How sweet the name of Jesus sounds." "Jesus, Jesus, Jesus, sweetest name I know."

Jesus cares; Jesus understands. Jesus experienced the abysmal impact of loneliness. Just when He needed His friends and disciples the most—when He was impaled on that cruel cross—they forsook Him and fled. Judas betrayed Him with a kiss. None of them would stay awake during His vigil in dark Gethsemane. And then on the cross, the Father turned His back on the Son. Talk about loneliness! In the awesome agony of that excruciatingly lonely moment, our Lord literally screamed aloud, "My God, my God, why hast thou forsaken Me?"

No human words can describe His loneliness on the tree. It is no wonder that He is now able to empathize and sympathize with us in our loneliness. Jesus has felt the pain we feel—and infinitely worse because He "became sin for us that we might become the righteousness of God through him." There is a real sense in which Jesus does feel the pain you feel. He sympathizes with you in your loneliness. He enters into our struggle with loneliness and isolation.

And He goes beyond sympathy to empathy. Sympathy is defined as feelings of pity for another person, but empathy goes far beyond mere feeling sorry for a person, pity. Empathy means actually to feel *with* and become involved with another. The perfect picture of empathy is found in matthew 9:35:

> But when He saw the multitudes he was moved with compassion on them, because they fainted, and were scattered abroad, as sheep having no shepherd.

The phrase "moved with compassion" literally means that *his heart went out to them.* He was caught up in their sickness and suffering. He was saddened because of their sins. His was and is a divine empathy.

Paul capsulated His empathy in Philippians 2:

> Who, being in the form of God, thought it not robbery to be equal with God: But made himself of no reputation, and took upon him the form of a servant, and was made in the likeness of men: And being found in fashion as a man, he humbled himself, and became obedient unto death, even the death of the cross (vv. 6–8).

And James wrote:

> Behold, we count those blessed who endured. You have heard of the endurance of Job and have seen the outcome of the Lord's dealings, that the Lord is full of compassion and is merciful (5:11, NASB).

Jesus sympathizes *and* empathizes with us. He hurts with us. One of the early church leaders believed in an idea called patripassionism. It meant that while the Son was on the cross, the Heavenly Father suffered with Him. For surely we know that God the Son has suffered for us and even now suffers with us.

Jesus has incomparable compassion, standing nearby to comfort and cheer. Many years ago it was a custom for mothers to say to their hurting, injured children: "Let mama kiss it and make it well." Beloved, that's what Jesus does! He kisses us through the Spirit and makes us well.

Many of us have tried every avenue and outlet but Him. Folks have tried alcohol, drugs, sex, gambling, expensive hobbies, material possessions, and a thousand other pursuits. Nothing will fill the emptiness of the heart until Jesus Christ is invited in. With Him you need never be lonely. He will keep you company morning, noon, and night. He will sit with you in your sicknesses, ease your suffering, bind up your wounds, dry your tears ... and help you to open yourself to include others in your life. He will lift you from loneliness to love and lilting life in Him.

> There's within my heart a melody;
> Jesus whispers sweet and low,
> "Fear not, I am with thee, peace, be still,"
> In all of life's ebb and flow.
>
> All my life was wrecked by sin and strife,
> Discord filled my heart with pain,
> Jesus swept across the broken strings,
> Stirred the slumb'ring chords again.
>
> Tho' sometimes he leads thro' waters deep,
> Trials fall across the way,
> Tho' sometimes the path seems rough and steep,
> See his footprints all the way.
>
> . . . .
>
> Jesus, Jesus, Jesus, Sweetest name I know,
> Fills my ev'ry longing, Keeps me singing as I go.
>
> —Luther B. Bridgers

"Surely the Lord is in this place." He understands your loneliness, and He has promised to stay with you while you are *tracing the rainbow through the rain.*

4
Tracing the Rainbow Through the Rain: Impulsive Behavior

Impulsive Behavior

Matthew 6:19-24

19 Lay not up for yourselves treasures upon earth, where moth and rust doth corrupt, and where thieves break through and steal; 20 But lay up for yourselves treasures in heaven, where neither moth nor rust doth corrupt, and where thieves do not break through nor steal: 21 For where your treasure is, there will be your heart also. 22 The light of the body is the eye: if therefore thine eye be single, thy whole body shall be full of light. 23 But if thine eye be evil, thy whole body shall be full of darkness. If therefore the light that is in thee be darkness, how great is that darkness! 24 No man can serve two masters: for either he will hate the one, and love the other: or else he will hold to the one, and despise the other. Ye cannot serve God and mammon.

Visualize this scene. A Christian couple is at home going over the bills. This couple ordinarily has smooth sailing in their marriage. Because of tiredness and pressing bills, Bill and Jane begin to become testy with each other. Before long they are yelling at each other—behavior that is totally uncharacteristic of their relationship.

Later, Bill and Jane make up with tears, and Bill, shaking his head in disbelief as Jane dabs her eyes with a tissue, apologizes

"Honey, I'm sorry. I just don't know why I do like that." Jane answers tearfully, "Darling, I'm so sorry that I called you those silly names. Please forgive me." But why do Bill and Jane act like that?

Ron is a faithful deacon in his church. His church activities are a blessed relief to him after the pressures of the office. In heavy traffic he is driving home from work. He is a representative of his Lord Jesus Christ.

Ron is driving the best he can, but an impatient driver is tailgating him. The tailgating continues for miles, it seems. All the while Ron is fuming and turning red around the collar. Then Mr. Tailgater passes and screams unintelligibly at Ron. Ron, the ambassador for Christ, yells back: "You stupid jerk, why don't you learn how to drive? You dummy!" Why does Ron act like that?

Have you ever had those impulses—or worse? "Why do I do what I do?" is an age-old question. Impulsive behavior is sometimes understandable in the unregenerate, but why do genuine followers of Christ think, speak, and act inconsistently with the gospel of their Lord?

The Apostle Paul struggled with this dilemma. Yes, Paul, the superlative missionary who carried the gospel, either in person or by letter to the entire known world. Yes, Paul who wrote thirteen books of the New Testament. Yes, Paul, the Christian martyr who lost his head on a Roman chocking block because he had preached the Word of the Lord without fear or favor.

> For the good that I would I do not; but the evil which I would not, that I do (Rom. 7:19).

How many times have you asked yourself, *Why did I do that? Why did I lose my temper? Why did I laugh at an off-color story? Why did I spank my child because I was angry? Why did I indulge myself in that moment of gossip?* Why? Why? Why?

Deep within us there seems to be a mechanism which drives us to continue doing (and thinking and saying) what we do not really want to do. How can we isolate this impulsive behavior and deal with it?

Years ago our denomination sponsored simultaneous revivals, and the watchword was: "Christ is the Answer." And for a fact He is! And He has the answer to our impulsive behavior.

In His Sermon on the Mount, He goes to the root of the matter and deals with our entire being: our affections (our hearts), our attitudes (our minds), and our actions (our wills). In a moment I am coming to His premier teachings about our life-styles, our impulsiveness, our contradictions.

There is a chain reaction in that our affection affects our attitudes, and our attitudes obviously affect our actions. So, why do we do what we do? We move in the direction of an answer by making a platform of the following premise: What we do is determined by what we think and what we think is determined by where our hearts are (our affections are)! This goes straight to the core of impulsive behavior.

We not only act impulsively, but we buy impulsively. Check your home sometime and catalog the unused items you bought on impulse. No wonder so many people are in trouble credit-wise. They all too often buy goods which are absolutely unnecessary for their comfort and pleasure.

An unknown author wisely wrote:

> Sow a thought, reap an act;
> Sow an act, reap a habit;
> Sow a habit, reap a character;
> Sow a character, reap a destiny.

That's how vital our thoughts are!

We think evilly or wrongfully and fly off the handle. Our thoughts all too often are inconsistent with the mind of Christ. So, many of us go through life frustrated and defeated in the Christian walk. Let me repeat for emphasis: What we do is determined by what we think, and what we think is determined by where our hearts are.

In this premise we discover our basic problem. Before the fall in Genesis 3, the proper order of decision-making was first the mind, then the emotions, then the will. But now, under sin, mankind has subtly reversed God's divine order of making decisions. Satan does not appeal to our minds initially. Where does he probe with his crafty guile? At our emotions, at our hearts. Why do I do what I do? Because I am a sinner, even though a saved sinner, and too often I make my decisions beginning with my *heart* instead of beginning with my *head*.

Let me put it like this. Our *admiration guides our affection*. Our *affection then governs our attitude*. Consequently *our attitude guarantees our action*. This affects all three areas of our being— our soul; the heart—the affections. Our spirit, the mind—the attitude. Our bodies, our wills—and our physical actions. Why do we do what we do? First . . .

Our Admiration Guides Our Affection

19 Lay not up for yourselves treasures upon earth, where moth and rust doth corrupt, and where thieves break through and steal: 20 But lay up for yourselves treasures in heaven, where neither moth nor rust doeth corrupt, and where thieves do not break through nor steal: for where your treasure is, there will your heart be also.

Admiration involves thinking highly of a person or object; It also implies an exaltation of the person or object admired. The wrong kind of admiration can turn into a form of idolatry. There is a sense in which we love the persons or objects we admire.

Jesus expressed it: "Where your treasure is, there will your heart be also." A person's treasure is what he admires. His affection is centered on his treasure, the person(s) or object(s) he ad-

mires. If one's treasure is in the world, one will love the world. I
am not referring to the globe on which we live—but the evil system
which Satan has let loose in the world.

In reference to this evil system of the devil, John the beloved
apostle warns us:

> Love not the world, neither the things that are in the world. If any
> man love the world, the love of the Father is not in him. For all
> that is in the world, the lust of the flesh, and the lust of the eyes,
> and the pride of life, is not of the Father, but is of the world. And
> the world passeth away, and the lust thereof; but he that doeth the
> will of God abideth for ever (1 John 2:15-17).

It all begins with our admiration, our affection from the heart.

All Eve did was admiringly glance at what Satan, the serpent,
offered in the Garden of Eden. Her admiration guided her affection. In the first place, Satan was suave and debonair. Only after
God cursed him, did he crawl on his belly in the form of a snake.
Satan plucked Eve's heartstrings with his appeal. It started in her
heart. Then, her affection began to govern her attitude. The temptation worked into her mind, and finally her attitude guaranteed her
action. It was no surprise that she ultimately accepted the fruit and
ate it.

And the process was the same with David, a man after God's
own heart. Why, all he did was take an admiring glance at Bathsheba while she bathed. Then his admiration guided his affection;
his affection began to govern his attitude. What was born in his
heart bore down on his mind. His attitude guaranteed his action,
and an adulterous affair with Bathsheba was the result, not to speak
of the crimes and sins David committed in connection with his lust,
including the orchestrated death of Uriah, Bathsheba's husband.

Why, why, why do we do what we do? Too frequently we
make our decisions by letting our hearts precede our heads. Jesus
declared: "Lay not up for yourselves treasures upon earth, where

moth and rust doth corrupt, and where thieves break through and steal: But lay up for yourselves treasures in heaven, where neither moth nor rust doth corrupt, and where thieves do not break through nor steal: For where your treasure is, there will your heart be also."

Many people spend all their time laying up treasures on this earth, ending up with nothing here or hereafter. The moths eat their tailor-made clothes; the rust corrodes their sleek, expensive automobiles. Thieves break and enter, stealing their priceless antiques and costly jewelry. Many a person who thought he could succeed by bowing down to the gods of this world has suddenly found himself with nothing. It is no wonder Jesus asked, "For what shall it profit a man, if he shall gain the whole world, and lose his own soul? Or what shall a man give in exchange for his soul?"(Mark 8:36-37).

Lew Sarett wrote of those preoccupied with material possessions:

> To him the moon was a silver dollar, spun
> Into the sky by some mysterious hand; the sun
> Was a gleaming golden coin—
>   His to purloin;
> The freshly minted stars were dimes of delight
>   Flung out upon the counter of the night.
> In yonder room he lies,
> With pennies on his eyes.

Our Lord opens with a negative word. "Lay not up for yourselves treasures upon earth, where moth and rust doth corrupt, and where thieves break through and steal." Our Lord constantly warms against earthly materialism. Don't let things possess you. Things never really satisfy. A new suit is all right for a few weeks—all your friends have already seen it by then and no longer make compliments. A brand-new automobile is OK until the new car smell goes away. A bouquet of flowers begins to decay before we ever get them delivered. "The world passeth away," wrote the Apostle John. Decay sets in moment by moment and hour by hour. There is change all around us. At times, nothing seems constant but change.

How foolish it is to set our affections on the possessions of this earth! Let Paul the apostle express it for us:

> If ye then be risen with Christ, seek those things which are above, where Christ sitteth on the right hand of God. Set your affections on things above, not on things on the earth
>
> (Col. 3:1-2).

I am a little amused at those who continually try to build up their self-image through their physical appearance. This world is passing away all around us. Many do not like to think on these truths because of impulsive behavior. They look at life through their emotions rather than their minds, making decisions based on the impulse of the split second. They are, as one singer put it, "hooked on a feeling."

There is also a positive word from the lips of our Lord. "But lay up for yourselves treasures in heaven, where neither moth nor rust doth corrupt and where thieves do not break through nor steal." Here is a word of encouragement about investments. We hear plenty about wise investments this day and time—IRA, tax shelters, commodities, stocks, bonds, insurance, mutual funds, you name it. Here Jesus gives exceedingly wise counsel about investments which will outlast recession, depression, war, and every imaginable "crunch."

Let me make a note here. There is nothing wrong with material possessions kept in proper perspective. Abraham was wealthy. Job was affluent before calamity struck, but the Word of God declares that "the Lord blessed the latter end of Job more than his beginning" (Job 42:12a). David certainly was not in the welfare line, and his son Solomon was considered the richest king of his era.

You have often heard, "Money is the root of all evil." That's an incorrect quotation of 1 Timothy 6:10, which states: "For the *love* of money is the root of all evil: which some coveted after, they have erred from the faith, and pierced themselves through with many sorrows." The *love* of money is wrong. Money can bless or curse, all according to what we do with it.

Many wealthy people I know are laying up treasures in heaven. In fact, many times it is those of us without a lot of material possessions who strive to lay up treasures on earth. The "have nots" often covet the possessions of the "haves."

It is all a matter of the affections. What our Lord forbids is the worship of our possessions, allowing them to preoccupy and consume us. Neither in the pursuit nor in the pleasure of things should they become our chief concern. I repeat: "Set your affections on things above, not on things on the earth."

If your treasure is deposited on earth, your heart will follow it. Likewise, if your treasure is deposited in heaven, your heart will follow it there. Why do we do what we do? Basically it is because we have laid up our treasures on earth, and consequently our admiration is guiding our affection which eventually governs our attitude—which inevitably guarantees our actions.

Our Lord presents the secret to becoming genuinely interested in Him and His enterprise. "Put your treasures in heavenly pursuits, and your heart will follow."

This is why so many people are committed to our fellowship of believers at First Baptist Church of Fort Lauderdale. They have put their treasure here. They have spiritually and materially paid the price for advancing God's kingdom through our church. It is not uncommon for our members to give their vacation or car money, which they have set aside, to a special missions offering. Their treasure is here, and so are their hearts.

If you put your treasure in a vacation home, your heart will be there. If you put your treasure in a beautiful body, your heart will be there. And if you put your treasure in the work of God, your heart will be there. I repeat: There is nothing wrong with a vacation home, a new car, or a beautiful body—unless they come before the Lord and His business. Jesus is speaking about priorities. During the Second World War, certain projects were labeled TOP PRIORITY. The kingdom of God has TOP PRIORITY with the devoted Christian who has his priorities straight.

Perhaps you are asking, "Why don't I care more about the work of God?" It may be that you have misplaced your treasure. Your heart is not caught up in the kingdom because your treasure is laid up in the pursuits of the carnal system around you.

Walter R. Bowie's poem, "The Empty Soul," speaks volumes:

> At the end will be but rust,
> Where earthly treasures are;
> They whose eyes are in the dust
> Will never see a star.
> They who came to Bethlehem
> And only dross have sought
> Will take away alone with them
> The emptiness they brought.

Since the fall, mankind has been governed by sinful desires, improper affections, and self-centered lusts. People are controlled by their emotions or desires. Such is the effect of sin on a fallen race.

How do we deal with this impulsive behavior? We pray that God will help us to be governed by His will rather than our emotions and feelings.

One of the real tragedies of sin is that it upsets God's order of decision-making. We do what we do initially because our admiration guides our affection. When this happens we then realize that

Our Affection Governs Our Attitude

22 The light of the body is the eye: if therefore thine eye be single, thy whole body shall be full of light. 23 But if thine eye be evil, thy whole body shall be full of darkness. If therefore the light that is in thee be darkness, how great is that darkness!

Why do we do what we do? Second Corinthians 4:4 gives an explanation: ". . . the god of this world [Satan] hath blinded the minds of them which believe not, lest the light of the glorious gospel of Christ, who is the image of God, should shine unto them." Satan has blinded what? "The minds of them which believe not."

Here Jesus speaks about eye trouble. The light of the body is the mind. Sin blinds those who are unbelieving and without Christ. Sin also dims the vision of Christians, although it can never totally blind them. Nonetheless, sin harms our vision of reality and values.

Yes, our admiration *guides* our affection, and then our affection governs our attitude. Sin blinds the minds of the unsaved, and it dims the vision of the saved.

The Lord illustrates this principle in verses 22 and 23. Sin blinds people's eyes to truths which should be perfectly obvious. Even as Christians try to accommodate their sins against the Lord, they often excuse themselves with, "Well, I just can't see that. I don't think God should expect such and such from me." The fact is: The rebellious Christian simply does not want clear vision. The unsaved person wants no vision at all.

Our sinful nature leads us to look at the world through distorted lenses. These warped lenses of sin make us sidestep responsibility, also causing us to bypass and ignore the truth. Aging is one example. Many people simply do not want to believe they are aging, that wrinkles are appearing, that the muscle tone is sagging, that skin blemishes and varicose veins are developing. Many an actress has gone insane or killed herself because youth was fleeting and the crow's feet were appearing. Yes, our bodies are deteriorating, and we might as well adjust to that manifest reality.

This spiritual myopia may spread to every nook and cranny of our lives. I am afraid many professing Christians are ignoring the clear truth of God's Word when they think about an illicit love affair. A large number of professing Christians are living together without the benefit of clergy. Years ago we called that, with disdain, "shacking up." Now many Christians are condoning the practice with alibis like this: "Why, if they truly love each other, there's nothing wrong with it."

But that's not how God feels about it. After all, He performed the first wedding ceremony in the Garden of Eden. He wants men and women to commit themselves to each other in the bonds of holy wedlock—"to live together after the ordinance of God." Even though they may claim commitment to each other before God, they ought to make it official before the state and mankind. Yet, we are living in a day when men and women are blinded to the clear-cut teachings of God's Word. Adultery and fornication are just as wrong today as they were when Jesus walked the Palestinian countryside. Why do so many Christians think living together is OK? Because they are making decisions from the emotions and not from the mind of Christ.

And this carries over to money. The stark fact is we own absolutely nothing. We will not carry one penny from this world with us. We will leave the scene exactly as we came in—naked and with nothing (see Job 1:21). Imagine it. All around us people are being governed by the stock market and the prime rate. We cannot carry that money with us, but we do not want to face it.

As a pastor I have conducted hundreds of funerals and followed hundreds of hearses in the funeral processions to the cemetery—but I have never seen a hearse with a "U-Haul" trailer behind it! The truth is: If we don't use it, we will leave it. We had best lay up our treasures in heaven. Then our treasures will have already preceded us. They will be waiting for us in heaven!

What one does is determined by what one thinks. What one thinks is determined by where one's heart is. *Our admiration guides our affection. Then our affection begins to govern our attitude.* Next

Our Attitude Guarantees Our Action

24 No man can serve two masters: for either he will hate the one, and love the other: or else he will hold to the one, and despise the other. Ye cannot serve God and mammon.

Thoughts. Then affections. Then attitudes. For emphasis I repeat the chain: Our admiration guides our affection. Our affection governs our attitude. Our attitude guarantees our action. They fit like the fingers in a carefully-measured glove.

Paul spoke of one deserter: "For Demas hath forsaken me, having loved this present world, and is departed unto Thessalonica" (2 Tim. 4:10a). Why? Because Demas had diverted his affections to the world and its cares. The attitude of his mind was altered, finally resulting in his leaving Paul. James 4:4 cries out: "Ye adulterers and adulteresses, know ye not that the friendship of the world is enmity with God? whosoever therefore will be a friend of the world is the enemy of God."

Having distinguished between two treasures and two eyes, our Lord now makes the distinction between two masters—God and mammon. The key word here is *serve.* "No man can *serve* two masters." Serve in this context means slavery. Why can't we serve two masters? Because their orders are diametrically opposed. One commands us to walk by faith; the other by sight. Jesus made it plain: We cannot serve two overlords. Those who serve God think, live, speak, and act by faith. Those who strive to please men alone walk by sight.

Mammon, most commentators think, stood for the god of material possessions. Mammon was a personification of wealth. We will either serve God or the god of possessions.

One commands us to be humble; the other proud. One demands that we set our affections on things above; the other on things here upon the earth. One commands us to believe before we see; the other to see before we believe. "No man can serve two masters ... Ye cannot serve God and mammon," Jesus emphatically stressed.

This is also why the Lord Jesus drew the line with this statement: "He that is not with me is against me; and he that gathereth not with me scattereth abroad" (Matt. 12:30). There is no middleground here, no fence-straddling. Many people have tried to serve two masters, but it simply will not work.

Without our priorities in proper perspective, without the decision-making process in spiritual sequence, and without clear vision, we can become slaves to the things which were intended to serve us. These earthly things meant for our benefit and good can become our deities. We can begin to build our lives around them. I like golf, but I have not let it master me. Many men and women are mastered by golf. It becomes the controlling force of their lives. Name it—hunting, fishing, business, clubs, fund raising, cars, boats, jewelry, antiques, eating, drinking—and it can become a minor deity.

I heard of a farmer who stayed away from church all during the fall and winter because he was afraid the pine needles on his acreage would catch afire and burn his property. He stayed right there every minute worrying over the slim prospects of a fire. He was blessed with huge acreage, pine trees, natural resources, and 500 head of cattle, but he never trusted God with them. His attitude about life was reflected when the spring arrived. He returned to church and would often ask the treasurer to change a one dollar bill for him so he could give *a quarter* in the collection to show his gratitude to God! That's a true story!

With a self-serving attitude, we end up serving dumb idols. That farmer did, and his life was wizened and spiritually impoverished. That happens because we reverse God's decision-making order. We become pitiful beggars, groveling before the pathetic thrones of materialistic idols. We become mastered by our appetites and become slaves to our possessions. Our goods become our gods! What a tragedy!

The worst detriment to the cause of Christ is God's people holding onto the world with one hand and to Him with the other. Many of us are spiritual schizophrenics, trying to live with dual life-styles and personalities. The disoriented Christian is miserable. The world looks at the backslidden, idolatrous believer and thinks he has never been saved!

Mahatma Gandhi, had he become a Christian, could have won millions of Indians to Christ. Perhaps no one man has had more impact on his country than Gandhi did on India. Late in his life he observed, "I would have become a Christian had it not been for Christians." What an indictment of unconcerned Christianity!

Now, the question is no longer why but *what*. What can you and I do about this impulsive behavior? What can we do about this maddening inconsistency, this ride on a spiritual see-saw? Up and down. Up and down.

This sounds so simplistic—but it works. *We can repent*. And what is repentance? It is a change of mind which affects a change of heart that affects a change of volition. We do what we do because we have been making our decisions in the wrong processes, and we must willingly change our minds—repent. Here I am not speaking about repentance in connection with salvation, unless, or course, you are not a Christian. But Christians are commanded to repent. "Repent; or else I will come unto thee quickly, and will fight against them with the sword of my mouth" (Rev. 2:16; see also

Rev. 2:5, Rev. 3:3,19). Believers are continually called on to change their attitudes and their minds.

To this day there is a difference of opinion about the true spiritual condition of the Prodigal Son when he left home. Was he saved or lost? Was he merely a backslider or was he unregenerate? Many are inclined to believe that he presents a picture of the backslider who falls out of fellowship with his Heavenly Father, but I am not going to split hairs.

What counts most of all is that the Father was willing to receive his wayward son. Luke 15 deals arrestingly with three parables—first, the story of the lost sheep; second, the story of the lost coin; and third, the story of the Prodigal (or lost) Son. After the boy traveled to that "far country," he dissipated his resources. That is often the case of a country boy who goes away to "the big city." He wants to do everything and buy everything in sight.

> And when he had spent all, there arose a mighty famine in that land; and he began to be in want. And he went and joined himself to a citizen of that country; and he sent him into his fields to feed swine. And he would fain have filled his belly with the husks that the swine did eat: and no man gave unto him. And when *he came to himself* [author's italics], he said, How many hired servants of my father's have bread enough and to spare, and I perish with hunger! I will arrise and go to my father, and will say unto him, Father, I have sinned against heaven, and before thee, And am no more worthy to be called thy son: make me as one of thy hired servants (Luke 15:14-19).

Down in that hog pen, that boy was really asking, *Why did I do this? Why did I act like this?* His admiration had guided his affection; his affection had governed his attitude; and his attitude had guaranteed his action. As a result he was eating swine feed instead of a sweet feast with his father. Right there in that sty, he repented: "I will arise and go to my father, and will say unto him, Father, I have sinned against heaven, and before thee" (v. 18). That was a clear-cut statement of repentance. How was he enabled to make a stand? The previous verse indicates: "And when he came to himself, he said. . ." Only by that realization was he able to repent.

He changed his mind. When he changed his mind, his volition—his will—changed. The remainder of the parable (vv. 20-32) details his going home, his heartfelt reception by his father, and the resentment of his older brother.

Size up the ingredients of the Prodigal's odyssey. He regretted his deed. He blamed himself for his sin. He acknowledged his father's right to be displeased, confessing, "I am no more worthy to be called thy son" (v. 21*b*). He had already resolved to make it right before leaving the swill and the swine.

What can we do about our impulsive behavior? How can we do away with having to ask ourselves the embarrassing question, *Why did I do that?* Regret your impulsiveness. Lay all of your impulses at the feet of Jesus. Acknowledge your sin of impetuosity. Recognize that God has a right to be displeased. Vow that you will stop letting emotions dictate rather than your mind controlled by the Holy Spirit. Allow the Word of God to shape every aspect of your life, including your decision-making.

The overriding question is: Whom will you serve? You cannot serve two. You will never have victory over impulsive behavior until the ownership of your life is straightened out. Does Jesus Christ have you? Repent and serve the living Lord only. Step by step you will trace the rainbow through the rain . . . to victory and triumph.

5
Tracing the Rainbow Through the Rain: Worry

Worry

Matthew 6:25-34

At least one sage has observed: "Worrying is a lot like rocking in a rocking chair—it will give you something to do, but it won't get you anywhere!" This crazy world is laden with situations and circumstances which lead many of us to a life of anxiety, anguish, and anticipation of the awful—worry!

Years ago a popular song asked the question, "Worry, why do I let myself worry?" Yes, why do I let myself worry? Why do you let yourself worry?

In a certain sense, the Christian—the born-again believer in a benevolent Lord—is under more pressure than the lost person. This is because of the spiritual stand to which the Christian is called. A pig is under virtually no pressure in the mud puddle. He merely settles in and becomes comfortable. On the other hand, a lamb feels sheer discomfort there! Why? It is against his nature.

Many Christians squander their time worrying about the past and the future, not to mention the present. They are guilty of presuming on yesterday and procrastinating on tomorrow. Because of this unChristian anxiety which often petrifies us, worry can lead to innumerable disorders—ulcers, colitis, rashes, facial tics, emotional disorders, "nervous breakdowns," strokes, heart attacks, and even death.

One unnamed philosopher expressed it:

To worry about what we can't help is useless. To worry about what we can help is stupid!

An unknown poet aptly put it:

Worry is an old man with bended head,
Carrying a load of feathers
Which he thinks are lead.

And one Chinese proverb summed it up:

The legs of the stork are long, and the legs of the duck are short. You cannot shorten the legs of the stork, nor can you lengthen the legs of the duck. Why worry?

We will never wrestle with worry and overcome it until we understand this overriding truth: Worry is not only frowned upon by God but is *forbidden* by Him! Many of us assume that God merely looks upon worry with a frown, but the fact is: He strictly forbids it in His Word.

Most every person, Christian and non-Christian, worries about worry, asking, "How can I wrestle with it and win?" How can I cope? How can I keep from falling apart?"

Our Lord and Savior addressed this exact issue in the Sermon on the Mount found in chapters 5-7 of Matthew. Our understanding Lord presents guidelines for grappling with and winning over worry. First of all, we have to:

Acknowledge the Source of Worry

Matthew 6:25-33

25 Therefore I say unto you, Take no thought for your life, what ye shall eat, or what ye shall drink: nor yet for your body, what ye shall put on? Is not the life more than meat, and the body than

raiment? 26 Behold the fowls of the air; for they sow not, neither do they reap, nor gather into barns; yet your heavenly Father feedeth them. Are ye not much better than they? 27 Which of you by taking thought can add one cubit unto his stature? 28 And why take ye thought for raiment? Consider the lilies of the field how they grow; they toil not, neither do they spin: 29 And yet I say unto you, that even Solomon in all his glory was not arrayed like one of these. 30 Wherefore, if God so clothe the grass of the field, which today is, and tomorrow is cast into the oven, shall he not much more clothe you, O ye of little faith? 31 Therefore take no thought, saying, What shall we eat? or, What shall we drink? or, Wherewithal shall we be clothed? 32 (For after all these things do the Gentiles seek:) for your heavenly Father knoweth that ye have need of all these things. 33 But seek ye first the kingdom of God, and his righteousness; and all these things shall be added unto you.

When Jesus declares "Take no thought," He does not mean to adopt a flippant, devil-may-care attitude which sidesteps and sneers at the serious issues of life. "Take no thought" in the original language meant "not to have a divided mind, a mind torn between two main objects." That is the condition of the backslidden Christian who, in the words of Billy Graham, tries to live "with one foot in the church and the other foot in the world."

James 1:8 refers to that kind of person: "A double-minded man is unstable in all his ways." Dear reader, worry is doublemindedness. It is faithless, foolish, frustrating, and futile to worry. When you make a habit of worry, you manifest your lack of faith and trust in the Lord who asks you to cast all of your care upon Him, because He cares for you (see 2 Pet. 5:7).

It is *foolish* to worry. Jesus teaches us to look at the birds of the air. They don't plant a crop, so they don't gather a harvest—and they don't have to maintain barns or storehouses. The Heavenly Father feeds them. And our Master asks all of us, "Aren't you better than they?" We are human beings gifted by God with intelligence—the ability to reason for ourselves and to make choices. In Christ, we are safe and secure. He has promised to care for us. "Just remember in His Word how He feeds the little bird; Take your burden to the Lord, and leave it there."

In this passage Jesus indicates that worry is sheer folly. It is significant that Jesus does not ask us to behold the mighty eagle as it soars "on the mountain high." Instead He uses the littlest of birds, a field sparrow, as an illustration. He takes note when that tiny bird is injured and falls to the ground. One of those teeny-weeny feathered creatures cannot hurt without the God of the universe stopping to express His heartfelt concern. The birds cannot store up food for the winter; they are pitiful and inferior alongside us. Yet, God provides for the little field sparrow's needs. Our Provident Lord cares infinitely more for us!

Birds are amazing creatures. I am always intrigued with them while visiting my in-laws at Pflugerville, Texas. Right outside my in-laws' dining room window hangs a hummingbird feeder. Those wee hummingbirds, two-and-a-half-inches long at the most, hover at the feeder, their wings beating ninety times a second. Once a year they leave that ranch and fly south over the Gulf of Mexico to Panama—and every year they return to that same ranch! How do they do that? God helps them do it! He created them with that precise homing instinct. Imagine it. And he cares far more for us.

Jesus reminds us that the Heavenly Father takes care of those birds. He has promised to watch over us without fail. "His eye is on the sparrow," dear Ethel Waters used to sing. "And I know He watches me." Our provisions, like the birds', come from the plentiful, protective hand of Almighty God.

> Said the robin to the sparrow
> "I should really like to know
> Why those anxious human beings
> Rush around and worry so."

Said the sparrow to the robin
"Friend, I think that it must be
That they have no Heavenly Father
Such as cares for you and me."

Worry. We worry over possessions, over provisions, even over God's promises. Worry indicates that God is not enthroned completely within us. When anxious, fretful worry pervades our lives, it tends to place a question mark over our profession of faith. It is foolish to worry.

And it is *futile* to worry. Jesus posed a piercing question, "Which of you by taking thought can add one cubit to his stature?" The Greek word used here for stature can also mean duration of life. Worrying is not going to help increase your actual physical size, your standing in the community, or your prestige. Jesus also indicated that worrying can add no length to your life. Think of it. Our times are in the hands of God. The Psalmist wrote that our days were already numbered before we ever lived a single one of them. Why worry then?

One reason we are consumed with worry is because of impatience. It's easy to preach and teach patience—waiting on the Lord to move in His own time—but it's exceedingly difficult to practice waiting. That's one of my pressing problems. I want answers now, action, results. I'm always in a hurry, but the Eternal God is not. He sees all of eternity with one bat of His eyes. We become fretful and impatient if there are not almost immediate answers and concrete results.

Jesus nowhere taught us to hurry and scurry, along with our worry. With His help, we must learn to wait on the Lord, and we must also recognize that it is foolish and futile, to no avail, to worry.

This reminds me of a parable about the clock. Sometimes clocks, especially grandfather clocks, have continued to run for a century or more—simply by ticking twice a second. Tick. Tock. Tick. Tock. Tick. Tock.

But suppose the old clock were given a human's brain and disposition. Instead of faithfully and loyally ticking without all kinds of doubt and questioning, the clock would begin to fret and worry. It would think to itself: *This' a drudge. It's not fair. All I do is tick and tock. I'm working myself to death. And the monotony of it all is devastating.* It would work itself into a frazzle.

The clock would begin to compute, putting a horrible strain on its works. Two strokes a second. Tick. Tock. One hundred and twenty strokes a minute. In an hour—7,200 ticks. In a day—172,800 ticks. Whew! The little clock tries an analyst, therapy, and pills.

Mercy, in a week—1,209,600 ticks. And in a year—62,899,200 ticks. And then the distraught clock starts to multiply by decades. The stress and strain are wearing away at the inward workings of the old clock as it counts the ticks, fretting with 628,992,000 ticks a decade. Finally, the old clock flies into a thousand pieces. Booiinnggg!

"It stopped short, never to go again...." Why? Because it worried itself into destruction. And the same is happening to real people all around us. They're coming apart at the seams because they are filled with fretfulness instead of faithfulness.

You remember the amazing account of John 11. Jesus received word from Mary and Martha of Bethany that their brother, Lazarus, was seriously ill (John 11:1-3). Yet, the Lord Jesus deliberately waited before going to Bethany. In fact, He tarried until Lazarus had died. (v. 11). When Jesus finally arrived at Bethany, Lazarus had already been dead and in the tomb for four days (v. 17).

Martha, all upset, hastened to meet Jesus, explaining, "Lord, if You had been here, my brother would not have died" (v. 21,

NASB). Later, when He came near Mary and Martha's home, Mary spoke those same words, "Lord, if You had been here, my brother would not have died."

What did Martha and Mary's words reveal? They had put their heads together and, in their frantic anxiety, had expressed puzzlement as to why Jesus had waited. When you meet two different people in two different places at two different times, and they speak the same words, you can readily recognize they have been together talking. They had worried themselves sick. They had asked each other, "How can Jesus do this? How can He procrastinate when we've called for Him? He must not care. We're among His best friends. Why, He's stayed with us. We've fed Him and his disciples so many times. We and Lazarus always welcomed Him with outstretched arms."

But Jesus had far better for Mary and Martha. Because of their shortsighted worry, they could not believe in miracles. When Jesus promised Martha, "Your brother shall rise again," she could not understand. She replied, "Lord, I know he will rise in the resurrection on the last day." Little did Martha realize the divine serendipity which lay ahead. Earlier, upon receiving news of Lazarus's sickness, the Master had explained to His disciples, "This sickness is not unto death, but for the glory of God, that the Son of God may be glorified by it" (v. 4, NASB). Jesus had known Lazarus's sickness would not lead to a final death.

Verses 34-44 record Jesus' weeping over Lazarus, His going to the tomb, and His calling Lazarus from the dead. "Lazarus, come forth," He shouted. And Lazarus did precisely that! Jesus always has the best in mind for us. Why do we fail to trust Him implicitly? Why are we impatient and fidgety about waiting on the Lord?

Throughout the Psalms we are admonished to "wait on the Lord." Psalm 130 is especially significant.

I wait for the Lord, my soul doth wait, and in his word do I hope.
My soul waiteth for the Lord more than they that watch for the
morning: I say, more than they that watch for the morning
(vv. 5-6).

What does that mean? The Psalmist waited on the Lord and
His promises far more than those who waited for the sun to rise.
Perhaps the Psalmist had in mind those who worshiped the sun or
those who were astrologers endeavoring to track the sun in its
course. "Tomorrow" is without a doubt the most popular song
from the musical *Annie*. It went, "The sun will come up tomorrow." Two facts are certain. Number one—we are going to have to
wait for the sun. We cannot hurry it up. It doesn't rise by our
watches. We must wait for it. Number two—it always rises. You
never wait for Old Sol in vain. If you wait on the Lord, you exceed
those who wait on the sun.

God is always right on time, and He always comes through;
no matter how desperate we may be, we never wait for Jesus in
vain. That's why it's foolish and futile to worry.

Worry never solves a single problem. In fact, it compounds
your problems. It is the most useless activity in life. It is futile.
What good does worry do? It does not empty tomorrow of its trials,
but it does empty today of its triumphs! Many live in the past, lamenting, "If only ..." They spend life crying over the proverbial
spilled milk. "If only I had married so and so ..." "If only I hadn't
married so and so ..." "If only I had gone to college ..." "If only I
had changed jobs when I had the chance ..." Those who live in the
past are crippled in the present and paralyzed in the future.

Innumerable people worry and wring their hands over tomorrow. "What will happen?" "Will my spouse leave me?" "Will I
lose my job" "Will the Russians control outer space?" "What will
happen to the prime lending rate?" "Will I have cancer?" These
folks are so obsessed with the future that the present marches on

by. I repeat: It is OK to plan for the future within reason. But it is not OK with God for you to worry over the past, the present, or the future!

It is not only foolish and futile to worry, but also downright *frustrating*. Jesus asked, "And why take ye thought for raiment?" In other words, why worry about the cut of your clothes? In eternity it will not matter whether your suit cost $79 or $579 or whether your dress was $109 or $1009. Why do you worry?

Our wise Lord then suggested we think about the lilies of the field. They don't toil. They don't spin. They don't punch a clock. They don't work in an office or factory, but let's gaze at their grandeur. "And yet I say unto you, that even Solomon in all his glory was not arrayed like one of these."

Jesus further wanted us to consider how they grow. The mystery of growth is one of the unsolved riddles of life. How does a tiny seed ultimately become a flower? How does a finite speck of protoplasm become a human being with all his intricacies of circulation, respiration, elimination—all the bodily processes and functions? In the winter the flower lies as if it were dead in the earth, covered with frost and snow. Yet, in the spring it sprouts up—stalks, leaves, blossoms, and all. And the same God of glory who oversees the lily, watches over you and me! Consider the lilies, how they grow. God does it! "They toil not, neither do they spin." They do not have to strain in order to produce growth and beauty. They are carefree.

Jesus observed that "even Solomon in all his glory was not arrayed like one of these." We cannot begin to visualize the opulent, lavish kingdom of Solomon—his resplendent crown, robe, and vestments; his palace with cedar furniture overlaid in gold; and his magnificent Temple, which had been the all-consuming dream of his father, David. All of that wealth, according to Jesus, pales into obscurity when compared to the radiance of a flower. All of Solomon's glory was from without. It was artificial, trumped-up, ostentatious. The lily's glory is within, a natural outworking of God's delicate touch.

Lilies, grass, and other vegetation do not last long. The moment we cut a flower, it begins to die. It is here today in all its gorgeous hues—it is gone tomorrow. Isaiah wrote: "The grass withereth, the flower fadeth: because the spirit of the Lord bloweth upon it . . . The grass withereth, the flower fadeth: but the word of our God shall stand for ever" (40:7-8). The flowers blossom and too soon die. But you are immortal. God cares infinitely for you. Worry, worry, worry—about the past, about the present, about the future. Hear me: It is foolish, futile, and frustrating to worry . . . and

It is *faithless* to worry. In the Sermon on the Mount, Jesus reminds His listeners that "if God so clothe the grass of the field, which today is, and tomorrow is cast into the oven, shall he not much more clothe you, O ye of little faith?" (Matt. 6:30). He chides us for not depending on Him, asking us to quit worrying about what we are going to eat and drink and wear.

And Jesus calls to memory the truth that the Heavenly Father knows we have these needs (see Matt. 6:31-32). "O ye of little faith," Jesus rebukes us. Worry, He teaches, reveals a lack of faith and trust in God's promise of protection and provision.

Genuine Christian living is nothing more than my "reacting." "We love him," wrote John, "because he first loved us" (1 John 4:19). Why do we love Him? Simple. Because He first loved us. He commands us: "Be ye holy." Why? "Because *I* am holy." The real test of spiritual maturity is not our actions—but our *reactions*. My main problem is not acting right but reacting right. This is the message of the Sermon on the Mount. Jesus deals almost exclusively with our reacting. Listen to His teaching in Matthew 5:38-46:

38 Ye have heard that it hath been said, An eye for an eye, and a tooth for a tooth: 39 But I say unto you, That ye resist not evil:

but whosoever shall smite thee on thy right cheek, turn to him
the other also. 40 And if any man sue thee at the law, and take
away thy coat, let him have thy cloak also. 41 And whosoever
shall compel thee to go a mile, go with him twain. 42 Give to
him that asketh thee, and from him that would borrow from thee
turn not thou away. 43 Ye have heard that it hath been said, Thou
shalt love thy neighbour, and hate thine enemy. 44 But I say unto
you, Love your enemies, bless them that curse you, do good to
them that hate you, and pray for them which despitefully use
you, and persecute you; 45 That ye may be the children of your
Father which is in heaven: for he maketh his sun to rise on the
evil and on the good, and sendeth rain on the just and on the
unjust. 46 For if ye love them which love you, what reward have
ye? do not even the publicans the same?

During Roman oppression a Roman official or military man
could command a Jew to carry his baggage or luggage a mile. That
was the legal standard, yet Jesus speaks of volunteering two miles
instead of the mile limit. Amazing! He teaches us to turn the other
cheek, and let's quit trying to skip around that teaching. He means
exactly that. Do not retaliate. It is better to allow your oppressor
another blow than to strike back. If a person sues you for one gar-
ment, grant him another one also. Now, all of this sounds crazy to
an unspiritual world, but it works. The acid test of our spiritual
maturity is not how we act, but how we react.

Now what does this have to do with worry? Worry is a reaction, a reaction to situations. Faith is a reaction to the Word of God.
If your life is governed by the Word of God, if you feed upon it—
and abide in Him as His words abide in you—then faith will become your automatic reaction to crisis or impending adversity. But
if you are controlled by circumstances and situations, then worry
will become your reaction to crisis. Worry is not an action on your
part—it is a reaction. It is only "natural" for a backslidden Christian to worry.

We cannot nourish worry and faith at the same time. How often we have prayed, "Lord, remove my burden. It's too heavy for me to carry," and then gone ahead and carried that heavy weight by ourselves. Why? Because we react from the standpoint of worry instead of from the stance of waiting upon the Lord.

When we worry, we are admitting, "God, I really don't believe you're big enough to handle my situation." What an insult to God! Maybe you protest, "But I don't know why God does things the way He does!" Frankly, I don't either. In fact, if I could understand it with my two-by-four mind, there wouldn't be much to His providence.

Jesus indicated that when we worry, we are acting like the Gentiles. Now most of us are Gentiles; I am not a physical Jew. Here Jesus was actually speaking about those without God, the unbelievers, the heathen. The pagans then and now live as though God does not exist. When you as a Christian worry, you are living like the lost. It is faithless to worry.

So, what distinguishes between the believer and the unbeliever ought to be reaction. Rather than worry, the believer is called on to wait upon the Lord. The committed believer trusts God in spite of what seems to be. One Christian minister who had suffered unjust persecution was asked, "How is the outlook?" To the question he answered, "The *outlook* is dark, but the *uplook* is wonderful." That's faith for you! The uplook is wonderful!

But you say, "I know all of these things, but I still can't get a handle on winning over my worries." Remember that it's not enough merely to acknowledge that the source of our worry is our doublemindedness, our divided minds. We must now

Apply the Solution to Worry
Matthew 6:33-34

Browsing the book stores is enjoyable, but at times it can become distressing. The stores are packed with volumes on anxiety, fear, stress, and worry. Most of these books claim to have answers. The sad awareness is: Most of them deal with the treatment of the symptoms and not the disease itself.

If you have a disease and only the symptoms are treated, you may improve for a while, but chances are the symptoms will manifest themselves once again.

First, we must grapple with the cause of worry before we can begin to effect the cure. Jesus certainly would not teach us not to worry without showing us how to keep from it.

A *valuable priority* is the first step in overcoming worry. What is this priority, this matter that ought to have first place in our affections?

> But seek ye first the kingdom of God, and his righteousness; and all these things shall be added unto you (6:33).

For most people the overpowering concern is, "I must first live ... I must first make money ... I must first clothe and feed and house my family." Jesus reverses this order and urges us to "seek ye first the kingdom of God, and his righteousness." Then, with the proper order and perspective established, "all these things shall be added unto you." All around us people struggle to provide for themselves and their families, but most of them have perverted priorities. Until, with the help of Christ, we rearrange our priorities, we will never "get it all together." Why? I repeat: because we are not seeking His kingdom first.

Henry Drummond, powerful preacher and author of *The Greatest Thing in the World,* penned these lines: "Above all things, do not touch Christianity, unless you are willing to seek the kingdom of heaven first." How many are dabbling with a form of Christianity without seeking the kingdom!

Seeking first the kingdom of God and His righteousness means a total surrender, a complete commitment. It involves acknowledging God's reign and rule over our lives. The kingdom must have a King. When we enthrone Jesus as King, a magnificent promise is ours: "All these things shall be added unto you." What does Jesus' promise imply? All our needs and all our tomorrows.

When we seek God first, we always find Him because, long before we ever thought about seeking Him, "The Son of man came to seek and to save that which was lost" (Luke 19:10). This is the valuable priority in overcoming our fears and worry. This is why the Psalmist could exult, "I sought the Lord ... and he heard me ... and he delivered me from all my fears" (Ps. 34:4). We will never, never overcome worry until this valuable priority has precedence in our lives.

A *vital principle* is also involved. Jesus closes out this section with reference to tomorrow:

> Take therefore no thought for the morrow: for the morrow shall take thought for the things of itself. Sufficient unto the day is the evil thereof (6:34).

Take no thought? Does this really mean we are not to think about it at all? Does this indicate that it is wrong to save money, have investments, or own insurance policies? No, that's not the point here. Jesus means not to *worry* about them. I love that old abbreviated expression, "Not to worry." That's all—not to worry. There is nothing wrong with seeking a sturdy shelter in the storm. Jesus is not forbidding that, but once you are safe and sound in the shelter, you should not continue to worry.

"Take no thought." Here again is reference to the thinking processes. The thrust of Jesus' teachings is: "Redirect your attention to the Lord." God places tremendous emphasis on our thought life. "As a man thinketh in his heart, so is he." Isaiah 26:3 consoles us: "Thou wilt keep him in perfect peace whose mind is stayed on thee, because he trusteth in thee."

There are three days in every week over which we ought not to worry—today, yesterday, and tomorrow. Those who fret about yesterday are guilty of pity. Those who fret about tomorrow are guilty of procrastination. Those who agonize over today may be distrusting of the Lord's goodness.

Some of us are promising God our tomorrows. Did it ever occur to you that God has never promised us tomorrow? And how could you promise God that which you may not have? This is exactly why Jesus admonished us, "Take therefore no thought for the morrow; for the morrow shall take thought for the things of itself. Sufficient unto the day is the evil thereof."

Tomorrow, tomorrow, tomorrow." "Tomorrow I'm going on a diet." "Tomorrow I'm going to quit smoking." "Tomorrow I'm going to begin tithing." "Tomorrow I'm going to make my stand for Christ." "Tomorrow I'm going to stop worrying." We put matters off until tomorrow because we hope they will go away and we won't have to face them—and tomorrow never comes!

When you are anxious about the future, you cripple yourself in the present. Oh, it is foolish, futile, frustrating, and faithless to worry. Here Jesus is teaching us to live one day at a time. Jesus was and is the world's greatest psychiatrist. This is the vital principle by which we can put the handle on worry. One day at a time. Julia Harris May wrote:

> Live day by day.
> Why art thou bending toward the backward way?
>   One summit and another thou shalt mount.
>   Why stop at every round the space to count
>   The past mistakes if thou must still remember?
>   Watch not the ashes of the dying ember.
> Kindle thy hope. Out all thy fears away—
>   Live day by day.

One step, one day—day by day with Jesus.

In this passage (Matthew 6:25-33) the Great Physician has plainly described for us the symptoms of this God-dishonoring and soul-paralyzing disease of worry. First, we are to acknowledge its source—it emanates from a divided mind. Once we realize this, we can apply the Physician's prescription to our worry. Believe it. It is possible for you to live above worry. How? Through a valuable priority of seeking first the kindom of God, and through a vital principle of living one day at a time. The bottom line is: We must deal with worry like we would any other sin—Confess it and forsake it!

Stop presuming on yesterday and procrastinating on tomorrow and "seek first the kingdom of God and his righteousness ... all these things shall be added unto you." Yield your frayed, tattered, worry-enshrouded existence to the Lord Jesus Christ. Climb out of that rocking chair. It doesn't get you anywhere anyway.

You will win over worry, and Jesus will stay right beside you. And as your worries are treated by the Great Physician, you will be *tracing the rainbow through the rain!*

6

Tracing the Rainbow Through the Rain: Depression

Depression

1 Kings 19:1-18

1 And Ahab told Jezebel all that Elijah had done, and withal how he had slain all the prophets with the sword.

2 Then Jezebel sent a messenger unto Elijah, saying, So let the gods do to me, and more also, if I make not thy life as the life of one of them by tomorrow about this time.

3 And when he saw that, he arose, and went for his life, and came to Beersheba, which belongeth to Judah, and left his servant there.

4 But he himself went a day's journey into the wilderness, and came and sat down under a juniper tree; and he requested for himself that he might die; and said, It is enough; now, O Lord, take away my life; for I am not better than my fathers.

5 And as he lay and slept under a juniper tree, behold, then an angel touched him, and said unto him, Arise and eat.

6 And he looked, and, behold, there was a cake baked on the coals, and a cruse of water at his head. And he did eat and drink, and laid him down again.

7 And the angel of the Lord came again the second time, and touched him, and said, Arise and eat; because the journey is too great for thee.

8 And he arose, and did eat and drink, and went in the strength of that meat forty days and forty nights unto Horeb the mount of God.

9 And he came thither unto a cave, and lodged there; and, behold, the word of the Lord came to him, and he said unto him, What doest thou here, Elijah?

10 And he said, I have been very jealous for the Lord God of hosts: for the children of Israel have forsaken thy covenant, thrown down thine altars, and slain thy prophets with the sword; and I, even I only, am left; and they seek my life, to take it away.

11 And he said, Go forth, and stand upon the mount before the Lord. And, behold the Lord passed by, and a great and strong wind rent the mountains, and brake in pieces the rocks before the Lord; but the Lord was not in the wind; and after the wind an earthquake; but the Lord was not in the earthquake:

12 And after the earthquake a fire; but the Lord was not in the fire; and after the fire a still small voice.

13 And it was so, when Elijah heard it, that he wrapped his face in his mantle, and went out, and stood in the entering in of the cave. And, behold, there came a voice unto him, and said, What doest thou here Elijah?

14 And he said, I have been very jealous for the Lord God of hosts: because the children of Israel have forsaken thy covenant, thrown down thine altars, and slain thy prophets with the sword; and I, even I only, am left; and they seek my life, to take it away.

15 And the Lord said unto him, Go, return on thy way to the wilderness of Damascus; and when thou comest, anoint Hazael to be king over Syria:

16 And Jehu the son of Nimshi shalt thou anoint to be king over Israel: and Elisha the son of Shaphat of Abelmeholah shalt thou anoint to be prophet in thy room.

17 And it shall come to pass, that him that escapeth the sword of Hazael shall Jehu slay: and him that escapeth from the sword of Jehu shall Elisha slay.

18 Yet I have left me seven thousand in Israel, all the knees which have not bowed unto Baal, and every mouth which hath not kissed him.

A strange fiction abounds today—that only failures become

depressed. In fact, the opposite is often the case. Winston Churchill, virtually a unanimous choice for the greatest world leader of 1900-1950, often fell into brooding periods of depression. For days on end his blue mood continued.

Toward his death, he became obsessed with the condition of the world. He often expressed his anxiety over the possibility of a nuclear holocaust. Even though a professing Christian, Sir Winston felt there was no hope for civilization.

William Cowper, who wrote hundreds of hymn lyrics and Christian poems, including "There Is a Fountain Filled with Blood," was dogged by depression until his death. As a result of his depression, he became an opium smoker and prayed for deliverance. At times he would fall back on the drug, then tearfully repent. He not only suffered physically but also mentally and spiritually.

Even though he was convinced that Jesus Christ could "save to the uttermost," he struggled with the assurance of his salvation, seldom ever feeling confident. He often begged and pled for assurance that he was truly "bound for the promised land."

In distress over his backslidings, he penned these incredibly touching lines:

> There is a fountain filled with blood
> Drawn from Immanuel's veins;
> And sinners plunged beneath that flood,
> Lose all their guilty stains:
> Lose all their guilty stains,
> Lose all their guilty stains;
> And sinners plunged beneath that flood,
> Lose all their guilty stains.
>
> The dying thief rejoiced to see
> That fountain in his day;
> And there may I, though vile as he,

Wash all my sins away:
Wash all my sins away;
Wash all my sins away;
And there may I, though vile as he,
Wash all my sins away.

His was a tortured, pain-wracked life, but somehow I believe we will meet William Cowper in heaven.

Depression is no respecter of persons. The fact is, however, that depression is more likely to oppress those who are creative, intelligent, and sensitive to the contradictions and sins of the human condition. If you claim to have no depression, check your pulse. Chances are you're dead and don't even know it!

Depression is common in a society which "pressure cooks" its inhabitants with anxiety and stress. One noted psychiatrist has written: "Today we can sum up depression as the result of certain biologic and social forces that, in a complex setting, act detrimentally on the person's nervous system function. The depressed activity in turn adversely changes the person's behavior, feeling tones, and thoughts. This totality of abnormal function constitutes a depressive illness."[1]

Ralph Speas observed in his book, *How to Deal with How You Feel,* that "depression is a general feeling of unhappiness. There are many and various causes of the emotional states we label with the word *depression.* Depression is related to other emotions. . . .

"Depression is sometimes related to physical causes. A hormone imbalance, wrong diet, lack of sleep, or physical trauma such as surgery can trigger depression. . . .

"I always ask depressed persons to see a physician for a physical examination if there are no obvious spiritual or emotional causes for their depression.[2]

God's Word is laden with cases of depressed persons. Nelson L. Price calls depression "fermented fear." He further points out the fact that eight million Americans (if not more) have depression deep enough to send them to the doctor or to cause them to miss work. In almost a litany, Price asks: "Can you imagine Moses depressed? ... Can you imagine Jeremiah depressed? ... Can you imagine Jonah depressed? ... Can you imagine John the Baptist depressed? ... Abraham in Canaan when the famine came, Moses at Meribah when there was no water, Job scraping his skin ulcers, and Peter locked in an upper room attest to the generality of depression."[3]

And there was Elijah. We can wear out adjectives on that mighty prophet, one of only two men in history who were translated straight into heaven. The other was Enoch who "walked with God: and he was not; for God took him." (Gen. 5:24). Few men in history have risen to the achievements or successes of Elijah. Recall that Elijah and Moses appeared on the Mount of Transfiguration when Jesus was transfigured (see Matt. 17:1-8). Think of it. God Almighty chose Elijah, of all His servants, to represent the prophets of the Old Testament at the Transfiguration!

Elijah was, to use the old cliché, "sitting on top of the world." In the name of Jehovah, Elijah could pronounce a drought, and the land would dry up. He could call forth the dead unto life, as in the case of the widow's son in Zarephath. And he called down fire in opposition to the false prophets of Baal on Mount Carmel. He had marched from conquest to conquest and triumph to triumph. And then it happened.

He fell into a deep depression. If you are an adult, you have heard it called that a thousand times, haven't you? I wonder if there is any such thing as a shallow depression. When depression surrounds you, it always feels *deep*. Winston Churchill called it "a black dog" which followed him around, nipping at his heels.

In spite of Elijah's extraordinary power with God, James in the New Testament wrote:

Elias [Elijah] was a man subject to like passions as we are, and he prayed earnestly that it might not rain: and it rained not on the earth by the space of three years and six months. And he prayed again, and the heaven gave rain, and the earth brought forth her fruit (James 5:17-18).

How can we defeat the dark cloud of depression? Yes, it is true that a number of people are depressed by biochemical changes in their bodies resulting in a physical cause of depression, and not merely an emotional or spiritual impetus. Yet, innumerable sufferers of depression have a kinship with Elijah in his virtually suicidal depression.

In order to deal with and defeat depression, we must begin by noting its sources and its symptoms—and then, most importantly, its solutions.

Sources of Depression

One of the primary sources of depression is *forgetfulness*. The Word of God records:

1 And Ahab told Jezebel all that Elijah had done, and withal how he had slain all the prophets with the sword. 2 Then Jezebel sent a messenger unto Elijah, saying, So let the gods do to me, and more also, if I make not thy life as the life of one of them tomorrow about this time. 3 And when he saw that, he arose, and went for his life, and came to Beersheba, which belongeth to Judah, and left his servant there.

We must recall that Elijah had just come down from the mountain top of miraculous victory. God had answered with fire! And then Elijah had confronted wicked King Ahab. The preceding verses of chapter 18 state:

41 And Elijah said unto Ahab, Get thee up, eat and drink; for there is a sound of abundance of rain. 42 So Ahab went up to eat

and to drink. And Elijah went up to the top of Carmel; and he cast himself down upon the earth, and put his face between his knees, 43 And said to his servant, Go up now, look toward the sea. And he went up, and looked, and said, There is nothing. And he said, Go again seven times. 44 And it came to pass at the seventh time, that he said, Behold, there ariseth a little cloud out of the sea, like a man's hand. And he said, Go up, say unto Ahab, Prepare thy chariot, and get thee down, that the rain stop thee not.

The key to Elijah's victory was that he had believed God, in spite of what appeared to be. As Martin Luther, the founder of the Protestant Reformation, expressed it: "Miracles take place, not because they are performed, but because they are believed." Like other powerful heroes and heroines of the faith, Elijah had believed God explicitly and implicitly.

But within the span of a few verses, Elijah seems to do a complete flip-flop. Once triumphant, he soon is cowed down, panicky and fearing for his life. What does his descent into depression imply for us? That the most dangerous time in the life of a believer is immediately after a victory, a triumph.

Elijah may have thought that yesterday's victories would suffice for today's commitments. He may have forgotten that we must have a day-by-day experience with the Lord. To me, this is often the primary source of depression in the life of a Christian—forgetfulness, failing to remember the power and promises of the God who "hath brought us safe thus far." It is as though we are smitten with spiritual amnesia. On the mountain top one minute—down in the valley, "The Slough of Despond," the next. How many of us Christians have a chills-and-fever experience! Flying high one day, shot down the following day.

Elijah heard that Jezebel, that venomous priestess of Baal, wanted him dead. Elijah changed almost instantly from a roaring lion to a pussycat afraid of a mouse! This was the same stalwart of God who, only hours before, had supervised the slaying of the false prophets of Baal. Elijah turned and "hightailed" it! He turned his eyes away from the God of glory and fixed them on an evil empress. He simply forgot that God was on the scene, that God had not changed, that God was still making His omnipotent power available.

Face it. Many of us fall into moods of depression—even manic-depressive mood swings—for this exact reason. We have a tendency to forget. Forgetfulness. Every believer has seen God come through on a mountain top. A loved one was miraculously healed through prayers of intercession. A job was found when it seemed none were in the offing. You were snatched from the jaws of death by manifest divine intervention. You were about to lose your mortgage, and an unexpected sum of money arrived. You were terrified because of a business appointment, and God gave you an unusual ability to communicate and cope. If you have been a Christian for any length of time, the Lord has escorted you to the mountain top. As it were, you have seen Him transfigured—and your life has also been transformed.

Yet, let a crisis come along—when a "Jezebel" threatens you—you run like Elijah. What a tragedy! How did you forget that God was with you? How could you possibly forget? It does not make sense. And that is the case. Such forgetfulness is senseless, foolish, and smacks of unbelief.

Poet Laureate of Great Britain during the reign of Victoria, Rudyard Kipling, penned these dramatic lines:

> The tumult and the shouting dies;
>   The captains and the kings depart—
> Still stands Thine ancient sacrifice,
>   An humble and a contrite heart.
> Lord God of Hosts, be with us yet,
>   Lest we forget—lest we forget!

Another source of depression is *fear*. Why did Elijah run? He beat a hasty path for safety because of fear which overcame him. Let's face it. He became afraid of Jezebel. Only hours before, Elijah had virtually sneered in her painted face. Remember that fear is not an action—it is a reaction. The prophet had won a resounding victory. How? By faith as he had "reacted" to God's commands and Word.

"Fear causes us to lose our perspective," comments Nelson Price. "Of course, the God of the universe is bigger than the cause of our fear. But when we focus on our fear and forget Him, the relativity is lost. An inordinate preoccupation with fear distorts reality. It is smart to back off and evaluate what is happening as unemotionally as possible. Feed your mind on fear-defensive facts. Let your mind bask in the magnificence and might of God. Readjust your perspective."[4]

But now fear had set in. It had stupified the prophet of God. Fear is a reaction—not an action—to the threat of danger and pain, whether real or imagined. Faith is a reaction to the Word of God. When the crisis comes, when Jezebel cackles and threatens our doom, if our lives are governed by situations and circumstances, our reaction will be fear—gnawing, numbing, bone-chilling fear. Fear that causes the pulse to race, the palms to sweat, the eyes to dilate, and the stomach to knot. Fear that sweeps over you and makes you nauseous.

On the contrary, if our lives are governed by Scripture, our reaction will be faith rather than fear.

In many respects, we are related to Elijah, many times more for our fear than our faith. Elijah reacted from fear rather than faith because he forgot. He forgot the source of his strength and sustenance, and so he feared. It was a gut-wrenching fear for his physical life.

Yet, there is another source of depression discovered in this text. It is *fatigue*. Overt sin is not always involved in the development of depression. Have you ever worked overtime on the job or perhaps at home on a special project, and you have labored 24, 48, or more hours virtually without sleep. Most of us have. Remember how you felt, *I believe I'm gonna die. I don't believe I can make it another moment.* Or you "crammed for exams" without cramming your stomach. You existed almost totally on caffeine in coffee or in those tablets called "No-Doz." Or have you ever driven a semi cross-country, pushing yourself to deliver that load of produce before it reached the spoiling point? Nearly all of us are familiar with the feeling of fatigue and tiredness—not only physically but also emotionally and spiritually. There you have a case for what they used to call "nervous exhaustion."

Sheer fatigue. The Scriptures declare: "He arose, and went for his life, and came to Beersheba, which belongeth to Judah." Elijah had spent innumerable hours atop Carmel. The emotional stress is almost impossible for us to comprehend.

Then, to add insult to injury, Elijah ran from Jezreel to Beersheba, a distance of 200 miles! Marathons and 10-K runs are in vogue today, but Elijah's Marathon retreat from Jezebel must have set the record. He was totally exhausted (and there was no Gatorade!). No wonder he collapsed into a shriveled heap!

In this connection Brooks Faulkner makes a timely statement about Elijah's exhausted condition:

> Most of us know how Elijah must have felt. We can come close to the same panic that is prevalent in his speech to the Eternal the God of hosts. If he is "the only one left," he doesn't feel like sharing his frustration with the world. Especially is this true if he feels he has given his ministry his best shot . . . his best effort . . . his all. Is it any wonder that burnout is the closet sin of the minister? We don't want people feeling sorry for us. It is enough that we feel sorry for ourselves.[5]

Exhausted, physically fatigued, drained of energy, Elijah was a ministerial burnout for a time. And this is the source of depression for many of us, preachers and laypersons. Pressing schedules, burdensome responsibilities, lack of sleep, constant problem-solving, living in a fishbowl, as it were, keep us from thinking right and making proper decisions. Fatigue, then, is a leading source of depression.

And *failure* is another source of depression. Elijah had reached the pinnacle of popularity. Why, he was the mouthpiece of the true and living God, Jehovah. All he did was pray sixty-seven words, and the fire of God fell! But now Elijah felt he was a failure and that he was ready for death. In fact, he asked God to snuff him out. He was too cowardly and too exhausted to attempt suicide himself, but he had become propelled by a suicidal death wish.

All of these sources working together—forgetfulness, fear, fatigue, and failure—led him to frustration and a "give-up" attitude. Those factors collaborated, plunging him into depression and into the juniper-tree syndrome. All around us are modern-day Elijahs who are depressed for a combination of reasons. They forget the God who loves them with an everlasting love. They fail to remember even recent blessings and victories. Astounding, isn't it? Yet, they seem to forget totally the presence of God on the scene. If only they could remember the truth of the poet's words:

> I, God, enfold thee like an atmosphere:
>   Thou to myself wert never yet more near;
> Think not to shun Me; whither would'st thou fly?
>   Nor go not hence to seek Me: I am here.
>   —James Rhoades

Others often react to situations in fear instead of faith. They seem to bypass the stabilizing influence of God's steadfast promises:

For God hath not given us the spirit of fear; but of power, and of love, and of a sound mind (2 Tim. 1:7).

What time I am afraid, I will trust in thee. In God will I praise his word, in God I have put my trust; I will not fear what flesh can do unto me (Ps. 56:3-4).

And the angel said unto them, Fear not: for, behold, I bring you good tidings of great joy, which shall be to all people (Luke 2:10).

Fear should have no place in our lives if we are following in faith. John Donne (1573-1631), best known by "For Whom the Bell Tolls," was a Christian poet of remarkable insight. If only we would pray as he did:

> I have a sin of fear, that when I have spun
> My last thread, I shall perish on the shore;
> Swear by Thyself, that at my death Thy Son
> Shall shine as He shines now; and heretofore;
> And, having done that, Thou hast done,
> I fear no more.

Still others have wallowed in failure to the point of rock-bottom depression—even to impulses or suicide itself. It sounds too simplistic, but it is absolutely true: if you have Jesus Christ as your Lord and Savior, you are not a failure. Maybe you are a failure in your own eyes or from the standpoint of the world, but you yourself are not a failure. Let me quote a perceptive writer:

> *First, understand that there is a difference between failing in some activity and being a failure.* To fail doesn't mean you are a failure. What you are as a person is always more than what is involved in one activity or endeavor ... Thomas Edison was unsuccessful in the first ninety-six experiments in his attempt to invent the light bulb. An assistant commented to the inventor about this abundance of failure. Mr. Edison answered, "The work is not wasted. We know ninety-six ways not to do it."[5]

You are a failure in your own mind. God does not regard you as a failure if you are found in Him. Write this down. Inscribe it on the tables of your heart—none of us can learn to defeat depression until we recognize the sources of depression. Once he has done that, he can then realize the

Symptoms of Depression

> 3 And when he saw that, he arose, and went for his life, and came to Beer-sheba, which belongeth to Judah, and left his servant there. 4 But he himself went a day's journey into the wilderness and came and sat down under a juniper tree: and he requested for himself that he might die; and said, It is enough; now, O Lord, take away my life; for I am not better than my fathers (19:3-4).

There is a clear distinction between a source of a problem and a symptom of a problem. Our profoundest difficulty is that we try to treat symptoms instead of sources. A friend of mine lived in a housing project as a child. They had water tanks in the apartments but no means of heating the water. My friend's dad had an ingenius idea—except that it backfired. He would put an electric hotplate right underneath the tank, and they had plenty of hot water until ... one night the tank overheated and the popoff valve blew, letting loose a steady stream of water.

My friend, thirteen then, woke up to the spectacle of the apartment filling up with water and his dad trying to catch the torrent of water with a bucket. Can you picture that? Here was an inexhaustible supply of water pouring all over the apartment and a distraught dad frantically trying to cope with the symptoms rather than the source.

My friend rushed in and yelled, "Dad, Dad, that's not gonna work. I'll go get the building superintendent, and he'll turn the water off outside." Within a short time my friend had summoned the super, and the water was turned off at its source.

The lesson is apparent. Treat the source instead of the mere symptoms. Go to the root, the heart of the situation. Once these sources have plunged us into depression, certainly there are symptoms which demonstrate that we are depressed. Let me suggest a few quite obvious symptoms of this debilitating state.

The first symptom often is *detachment,* flight, withdrawal. Elijah left his servant and traveled a day's journey into the wilderness. There he sat down under a juniper tree. Isolation. Capitulation. Detachment. Elijah left those who loved and supported him. How often I have heard a spouse seeking to orchestrate a divorce by explaining, "I've just got to get away to myself. I gotta think." That sounds good . . . or does it? Sometimes that person is getting away actually to be with a paramour. Many times the person thinks it will help to withdraw. It might and it might not; it could lead to the breakup of a marriage that ought to stay intact. Many depressed persons want to stay in bed and do nothing, to withdraw from those who really know them and love them.

Remember that this is a symptom and not a source! It is not enough for us to tell the depressed person, "Just get up out of bed, and go on." Let me ask: "Do we get depressed because we are isolated or are we isolated because we are depressed?" My definite feeling is that detachment is a symptom.

Withdrawal for the right reasons is beneficial, unless it is overdone. Jesus withdrew with his disciples and at times by himself. But withdrawal in order to pity oneself or to make our family or friends feel bad or to express anger or to cop out of serving the Lord is downright sinful. Part of Elijah's motives were on target, but others were off the mark.

Another symptom of depression is *despondency.* The account further indicates that Elijah "requested for himself that he might die." In other words, he had a death wish, but he himself was not willing to carry it out. He asked the Lord to kill him: "O Lord, take away my life." Nearly every seasoned Christian has prayed like that at least once. "Lord, this is more than I can bear. No one understands. No one seems to care for me. No one appreciates my ministry. Lord, I'd be better off to leave this life. I'm so tired and worn out. Jesus, I can't carry on any longer." Confess. If you've been a Christian anytime, you have more than likely had those same pitiful sentiments.

Elijah was characterized by pessimism and an utter sense of hopelessness. Elijah, at least momentarily, had lost his will to live. He was almost as bad off as the fellow who commented, "I'd shoot myself to death, but I'd hate to waste a bullet." He was thinking in the wrong channels because of forgetfulness, fear, fatigue, and failure (he thought). His despondent mood was merely a symptom of a deeper problem. Are we despondent because we are depressed or depressed because we are despondent? Thinking positive thoughts, however good that is, will not overcome despondency and depression. Many untrained (and even the trained) people try to force positive thinking on those who are not able to act upon it. Positive thinking is not enough. *After the source is identified,* a Christian application of positive thinking will motivate the believer.

Another symptom of depression is *defeat.* "It is enough; now, O Lord, take away my life; for I am not better than my fathers." A stifling defeatist attitude had set in. "I'm no good," was the defeatist cry of poor Elijah. In essence, he was making the point to the Lord, "I've tried so hard, Lord, but I'm so inferior. I can't be compared with Moses or Abraham—or even any of my forefathers." Once again you must deal with the source. We are not depressed because we are defeated. We are defeated because we are depressed.

Yet another symptom is *deception.* Elijah, now detached and despondent and defeated, moans: "I have been very jealous for the Lord God of hosts: for the children of Israel have forsaken thy covenant, thrown down thine altars, and slain thy prophets with the sword; and I, even I only, am left; and they seek my life, to take it away" (v. 10).

There is a prime example of faulty thinking. Poor, pitiful Elijah. He was the only one left, so he thought. God emphatically answered that Elijah was deceived and dead wrong.

In verse 18 God reminds Elijah: "Yet I have left me seven thousand in Israel, all the knees which have not bowed unto Baal, and every mouth which hath not kissed him." Most of us are modern-day Elijahs, not in our power but in our paranoia. We have a persecution complex. Nothing's right. Everything's wrong. People are plotting against us. "Lord, I'm the only one who loves you in my church and in my community. I'm the only one who cares. Oh, boo hoo!!!" And then we add, "Even at that, I'm no good." Isn't that contradictory and plain stupid? If you're the only one who's living for the Lord, that ought to mean you're plenty good. You're spiritual. You're making a mark for Jesus. It doesn't make sense, does it? You're so dedicated and so consecrated and so committed, but at the same time you're a no-good, lousy wretch! His reasoning, like ours can be, was faulty and defective.

Remember that deception is not a source. It's a symptom. We do not become depressed because we are deceived. We are deceived because we are depressed. It is simply the symptom of the genuine sources of forgetfulness, fear, fatigue, and failure.

Still another symptom of depression is *defensiveness*. Listen to Elijah's pitiful cry: "I have been very jealous for the Lord God of hosts; for the children of Israel have forsaken thy covenant, thrown down thine altars, and slain thy prophets with the sword; and I, even I only, am left, and they seek my life, to take it away." Now he becomes defensive—"I alone am left." Here is total preoccupation with self. His eyes are only on his own problem. This is a bona fide symptom of depression. That is, the depressed person is only interested in the little world that is bounded on the north, east, south, and west by the perpendicular pronoun. That is the depressed person's obsession. Self. Ego. I.

The depressed person becomes defensive, edgy, and wrapped up in his feelings. He repeats, "Nothing matters anymore." In claiming he wants to be left alone, he is actually begging egotistically for attention. He has a psychological chip on his shoulder.

Let me recap the sources of depression. *Forgetfulness*. We forget who bought us on the cross; we forget our roots in Christ; we forget His past blessings; we forget the good and focus on the bad. We live as though God did not exist.

Fear. Why should we fear if God is with us? John wrote in his first Epistle: "There is no fear in love; but perfect love casts out fear, because fear involves punishment, and the one who fears is not made perfect in love" (1 John 4:18, NASB).

Fatigue. When we are worn out and exhausted, we must lean heavily on the Holy Spirit's strength. When fatigued we become vulnerable to the "slings and arrows" of the devil.

Failure. When we seem to fail, let us ask the question, "By whose standard of failure?" If you are endeavoring to serve the Lord, no matter the adverse conditions, you have not failed. Does God consider you a failure? The world considers the backwoods preacher a failure. If that pastor is faithfully ministering and holding forth the word of life, he is a resounding success. Failure in whose eyes? That is the question one must ask.

For the sake of the kingdom, do not try to treat the symptoms of depression—detachment, despondency, defeat, deception, and defensiveness. You will stay depressed for long periods of time unless you return to the sources of depression. Finally, and most importantly, let us note some

Solutions to Depression

Ironically, the first solution is *physical*. The Bible account continues:

5 And as he lay and slept under a juniper tree, behold, then an angel touched him, and said unto him, Arise and eat. 6 And he looked, and, behold, there was a cake baked on the coals, and a cruse of water at his head. And he did eat and drink, and laid him down again. 7 And the angel of the Lord came again the second time, and touched him, and said, Arise and eat; because the journey is too great for thee.

On the road to recovery from his depression, Elijah first slept and then ate and drank. This is tremendous biblical advice. Rest. Learn to relax. Lean on the everlasting arms. Eat enough to gain strength. We ought to have a balanced diet and sleep enough. Sleep needs, of course, vary from person to person. Edison, the genius inventor, slept no more than four hours a night, but he learned the wisdom of "cat naps" during the day. Eight hours seems right for most adults. Nine or ten, unless you have lost sleep for a couple of days, is probably too much. Heart specialists are now claiming that *too much* sleep can be just as bad as too little. Too much sleep does not properly make the heart work and the blood pump.

This part of the solution is physical. Many physically fatigued people may doubt their salvation because they so often think of salvation in terms of "feeling good." Fatigued people also put themselves in a vulnerable position before the devil and His cohorts. It may be that we have a biochemical need, and perhaps there is a chemical imbalance in our systems. Fatigue is one of the sources. Good health is certainly one of the solutions.

While the solution is physical, it is also *personal*. The account also states:

9 And he came thither unto a cave, and lodged there; and, behold, the word of the Lord came to him, and he said unto him, What doest thou here, Elijah? 10 And he said, I have been very jealous for the Lord God of hosts: for the children of Israel have forsaken thy covenant, thrown down thine altars, and slain thy prophets with the sword; and I, even I only, am left; and they

seek my life, to take it away. 11 And he said, Go forth, and stand upon the mount before the Lord. And, behold the Lord passed by, and a great and strong wind rent the mountains, and brake in pieces the rocks before the Lord; but the Lord was not in the wind; and after the wind an earthquake; but the Lord was not in the earthquake: 12 And after the earthquake a fire; but the Lord was not in the fire; and after the fire a still small voice.

In order to overcome depression, we must personally look at ourselves. We must ascertain where we are—and then assume responsibility. Instead of alibiing, "I alone am left," we need to admit, "I alone am responsible." This is a giant step toward defeating depression.

In verse 9 God asked an intriguing question. "Elijah, what are you doing here?" When I arrive in heaven, I would love to find out where God put the inflection in many of His questions recorded in His Word. I have always wondered where the inflection in God's voice was in this particular question. Maybe he asked, "What are YOU doing here?" "Elijah, of all people in the world, what are YOU doing here? You had such courage on Mount Carmel. You had such faith at the widow's home at Zarephath. I would have expected this retreat of anyone but you, so what are YOU doing here?"

Maybe the inflection was in another place. "What are you doing HERE?" "Of all the places one earth, Elijah, what are you doing HERE underneath this juniper tree? Out here in the middle of nowhere? What are you doing HERE?" Have you ever been in a place where you knew God didn't want you to be, and you heard that still small voice deep down inside asking, "What are you doing HERE?"?

But perhaps God put His inflection on still another word: "What are you DOING here?" Elijah, in that case, would have been compelled to reply, "I'm not DOING anything, Lord. I'm just feeling sorry for myself, wishing I were dead." Many of us lose our joy by DOING *nothing!*

What is the prevailing lesson? You cannot run from God. You cannot get away from "the hound of heaven." Francis Thompson, in his epic "The Hound of Heaven," wrote concerning his flight from God:

> I fled Him, down the nights and down the days;
>   I fled Him down the arches of the years;
> I fled Him down the labyrinthine ways
>   Of my own mind; and in the midst of tears
> I fled from Him, and under running laughter,
>   Up vistaed hopes I sped;
>   And shot, precipitated,
>   down titanic glooms of chasmed fears,
> From those strong feet that followed, followed after.
>
>   But with unhurrying chase
>   And unperturbed pace,
>   Deliberate speed, majestic instancy,
>   They beat—and a Voice beat
>   More instant than the Feet—
> "All things betray thee, who betrayest Me."

The danger of today's tranquilizer is that it simply puts off the day when we will have to face the foe. If you find yourself in depression, God is speaking to you: "What are you doing here?"

Do you hear that still small voice? The solution is personal. God speaks to you and me as He did Elijah:

11 And he said, Go forth, and stand upon the mount before the Lord. And, behold the Lord passed by, and a great and a strong wind rent the mountains, and brake in pieces the rocks before the Lord: but the Lord was not in the wind; and after the wind an earthquake; but the Lord was not in the earthquake: 12 And af-

ter the earthquake a fire; but the Lord was not in the fire; and after the fire a still small voice.

We are living in a day when people lust for the spectacular. They want to be struck with "an experience." They want to feel the cyclonic wind, hear and behold the earthquake, and view the fire. They long for spiritual pyrotechnics. They want a chills-up-and-down-the-spine experience. But God still speaks in that still small voice and says, "I'm not through with you yet."

Yes, we sometimes have to crawl under that juniper tree before we can hear God speak. The truth is: the most profound lessons are not learned on the mountain tops. They are taught us in the valleys—down under our very own juniper trees. There, by practical experience, we hammer out a life of victory. I personally never seem to learn a spiritual truth in the eagle's aerie, but always in the cardinal's nest down close to the ground. Not on the mountain top but in the valley, "valley so low." Longfellow must have had similar thoughts when he wrote: "The lowest ebb is the turn of the tide." An unnamed sage opined, "There has never been a sunset that wasn't followed by a sunrise."

The solution to depression is *physical* and *personal*, but it is also *practical*. God continued:

15 And the Lord said unto him, Go, return on thy way to the wilderness of Damascus; and when thou comest, anoint Hazael to be king over Syria: 16 And Jehu the son of Nimshi shalt thou anoint to be king over Israel: and Elisha the son of Shaphat of Abelmeholah shalt thou anoint to be prophet in thy room.

God gave Elijah an assignment. Elijah arose from his pallet of depression. He accepted the assignment and became busy for God. God gave him a job which involved other people. Here was a practical solution to depression. Elijah left his depression and moved on to the most marvelous days of his ministry. His depression was not a dead end. Neither is yours. Your blue mood may become the vantage point to the road that winds ever upward.

Many have remarked to me, "Why, I never thought of that." Simple, isn't it? Elementary, dear Watson—but so often ignored. Become involved. Accept an assignment from the Lord. The number-one deterrent to depression is soul-winning. Lead another person to Jesus and help rid him of his depression. The most glorious joy in all the world is to see a person saved and transformed by the Lord Jesus. We still reap what we sow. If you sow the seeds of joy in Christ, they will blossom into beauty. Cast your bread upon the waters, and it will return to you one hundred times over (Eccl. 11:1).

Consequently, we note that the solution to depression is three-fold. Physical, personal, and practical. You will never overcome depression until you personally trust God, until you are physically sustained, and until you become busy for God.

If the sources of depression are fear, fatigue, and forgetfulness, and failure, how do we treat them? We treat fear with faith. "Faith cometh by hearing, and hearing by the word of God (Rom. 10:17). There is the personal solution. Treat fatigue with rest. There is the physical solution. We treat forgetfulness by training ourselves to remember what God has done for us—and then plunging ourselves into His service. We treat failure by realizing there is success in Christ. Here is the practical solution.

Are you prone to moods of depression? Then God inquires, "What are you doing here?"

The last time we see Elijah in the Word is on the Mount of Transfiguration, gloriously being transfigured with the Lord Jesus Christ and Moses. He is no longer running from the Jezebels of this world.

Today perhaps you are running and finally find yourself under your own juniper tree. There you are moaning the blues. If you will only listen to that still small voice, God will speak to your heart. Stop looking for the wind, the earthquake, and the fire—the experience. I repeat: simply listen to the still small voice and begin to trust totally in Jesus.

First Kings 19:11 makes this observation: "Behold, the Lord is passing by." He is passing by at this moment, and He is the only solution to your depression. When we are under the juniper tree, he takes us by the hand and walks by our side, helping us in the process of *tracing the rainbow through the rain.*

7

Tracing the Rainbow
Through the Rain:
Improper Self-image

Improper Self-image

Exodus 3:11

And Moses said unto God, Who am I, that I should go unto
Pharaoh, and that I should bring forth the children of Israel out
of Egypt? (Ex. 3:11).

For at least two decades, counselors, psychologists, and psy-
chiatrists across the world have emphasized self-image. How does
a person feel about himself/herself? How does this influence attitudes, behavior, and life-style. And quite frankly, knowledgeable
Americans have often become tired of hearing "self-image, self-
image, self-image."

Especially was this self-image craze intensified by books like
I'm OK—You're OK by Thomas A. Harris, with assistance from
his wife, Amy. The "renewal" movement in Christian circles
placed considerable importance on self-image.

Really, now? How vital is the role of self-image in a person's
life? Thirty and forty years ago, Americans did not think in terms
of self-image.

Why bandy it about? Why not plunge directly into the subject
as it relates to none other than the premier lawgiver, Moses?

It was "business as usual" on the backside of the desert.
Moses led the nomadic life of a shepherd. This day was no different

from any other day, so Moses thought. Little did this roving shepherd realize all that was in store for him. It almost reminds me of Walter Cronkite's intoning, "And this has been a day like any other day, except *You Were There!*"

Imagine Moses' absolute amazement as he beheld a bush that continued to burn, yet was not consumed. From the bush came the voice of God Almighty, Jehovah.

It is understandable that human beings, freighted with guilt and sin, tend to cringe before God. What would you do if He spoke to you out of a bush in your back yard? You might scratch your head and begin babbling to yourself.

God spoke, as He had spoken before and as He would speak again. He delivered the command, "Moses, you will go to Pharaoh, and you will say, 'Let my people go.'" Moses' initial response was most revealing: "Who am I that I should go unto Pharaoh, and that I should bring forth the children of Israel out of Egypt?"

Who am I? That is an appropriate question for all of us to ask. Moses epitomizes a person who suffers from a poor self-image. Call it what you will—self-image, feelings about oneself, attitude, perspective about life, you name it.

Moses had known rejection. When God called him to a specific mission, Moses' impulse was to ask, in self-deprecation, "Who me? Who am I?" I do not believe, either, that it was a false modesty. Moses was petrified with a sense of unworthiness. Think, for instance, of Isaiah when he was in the Temple, and he saw "the Lord high and lifted up." What was his response to that encounter with the God of glory? "Woe is me, for I am ruined! Because I am a man of unclean lips. And I live among a people of unclean lips; for my eyes have seen the King, the Lord of hosts." (Isa. 6:5, NASB).

Even though awe, wonder, and maybe even fright were normal responses from people like Abraham, Moses, and Isaiah, all of them grappled with a common human condition. They felt inferior, not only to God but also to man.

Moses' inferiority complex was understandable. He was a Hebrew and had undergone persecution and ostracism because of his lineage. In Exodus 1, the Hebrews had multiplied thick and fast, and the midwives were doing a "land-office business." The new Pharaoh was deathly afraid of the Hebrews' becoming predominant. He appointed taskmasters over them to place them under hard labor. Pharaoh's plan was genocide—to enslave the Hebrews until they broke and finally died under the strain.

But listen to Exodus 1:12: "But the more they afflicted them, the more they multiplied and the more they spread out, so that they were in dread of the sons of Israel" (NASB). The more they were put down, the more they prospered. When you come down to it— because of his background and his lineage—there was no reason for Moses to have an inferiority complex. The Hebrews were winners. No matter what happened to them, they snapped back. They were resilient.

Pharaoh had commanded the Hebrew midwives to let male babies die in childbirth, but they did not abide by his macabre orders. Exodus 1:20-21 states: "And it came about because the midwives feared God, that He established households for them. Then Pharaoh commanded all his people, saying, 'Every son who is born you are to cast into the Nile, and every daughter you are to keep alive.'" (NASB).

Into that situation of doom, Moses was born. Fearing for his life, his mother put him in a wicker basket and set the basket afloat in the reeds (we used to call them "bullrushes") along the banks of the Nile. Every faithful Sunday School child is familiar with the story of Moses as a baby—found by Pharaoh's daughter, reared by her in the court of Pharaoh. She actually named him Moses which means "drawn out of the water."

When Moses grew up he became painfully aware of the plight

of his people. One day he saw an Egyptian beating a Hebrew. Moses made sure the coast was clear and then struck down his Egyptian taskmaster, killing him. Moses buried the Egyptian's body in the sand. His was not a premeditated act of murder—he was only trying to rescue one of his brethren. He saw two of his Hebrew brethren fighting the following day and tried to break it up. To Moses' chagrin he became aware that his murder of the Egyptian must have been found out, for the "offender" in the fight answered: "Who made you a prince or a judge over us? Are you intending to kill me, as you killed the Egyptian?" Then Moses was afraid, and mused, "Surely the matter has become known" (Ex. 2:14).

So, when Pharaoh heard of the killing, he sought to have Moses killed. Moses became a fugitive and settled in the barren desert land of Midian, now called Jordan. There Moses was offered hospitality by Reuel (Jethro) and was given one of Reuel's seven daughters, Zipporah, in marriage. They had a son and named him Gershom.

Then the stage is set in the Scriptures.

> 23 Now it came about in the course of those many days that the king of Egypt died. And the sons of Israel sighed because of the bondage, and they cried out; and their cry because of their bondage rose up to God. 24 So God heard their groaning; and God remembered His covenant with Abraham, Isaac, and Jacob. 25 And God saw the sons of Israel, and God took notice of them (Ex. 2:23-25, NASB).

So, Moses had no concrete reason to feel inferior. God had intervened for him repeatedly. And now God had spoken miraculously through the burning bush—burning yet not being consumed! Moses would overcome, but he had to grapple with his identity and had to answer the question: "Who am I?"

Many people, even professing Christians, spend their whole

lifetimes posturing from a low self-image. I am not so idealistic as to think that: in the reading of this brief chapter, a lifetime of building a low self-image can be translated into a positive, proper self-image—the image God wants us to have. But I am emboldened with enough faith to believe that, from this chapter, one can find direction in developing new thought patterns that can literally transform one's own self-image.

Proverbs 23:7 succinctly states the case: "For as he thinketh in his heart, so is he." I do not necessarily agree with every positive-thinking kick which comes along—unless, of course, it is rooted and grounded in the Word of God. But there is power in positive thinking, provided that positive thinking is linked with the possibilities in the Lord Jesus Christ.

First, Moses had to ascertain who he was—not merely a Midianite shepherd, not simply a tongue-tied, timid Hebrew. Moses had to recognize that the power of the Almighty was upon him, that Jehovah God had called him to a special commission, and that God would stand with him in carrying out that monumental task of leading the children of Israel out of bondage in the land of Egypt.

Today there is considerable emphasis on "imaging." How do you perceive yourself? Who are you? What are you doing? It's OK to sing "I'm Just an Old Chunk of Coal," if you add, "I'm gonna be a diamond someday." There is nothing wrong with being a chunk of coal if you trust God to make and mold you into that classy diamond. To use that hackneyed, but true, expression: "God ain't through with me yet." He is at work in our lives, pressuring these chunks until they are transformed. Moses and you and I are diamonds in the rough.

In order to work on a proper self-image, we must observe the real self. How do we image ourselves? Many of us image ourselves physically. Others, emotionally. A few of us image ourselves spiritually. Most people never realize their value. It is heartbreaking to hear a child of the King moan, "Oh, I'm nothing. I'm no count. I'll never amount to a hill of beans." That's tragic.

Many view themselves primarily from a physical standpoint. Why? Because they are prone to think in physical terms instead of spiritual. Too few of us see ourselves for who we really are—that is, from a spiritual standpoint. The pathway to proper self-image is begun when we realize who we are in actuality.

Paul wrote: "And the very God of peace sanctify you wholly; and I pray God your whole *spirit* and *soul* and *body* be preserved blameless unto the coming of our Lord Jesus Christ" (1 Thess. 5:23). We are made up of three parts (and I realize there is debate on this matter): spirit, soul, and body. We generally reverse the order in conversation. Most of us say "body, soul, and spirit." This is because subconsciously we are more body-conscious, and this is a portion of our problem with self-image. The natural, earthly matters mean more to many of us than the spiritual aspects of life.

Think about it. Many of us are obsessed with our bodies. Each day we spend immeasurably more time preparing our bodies than our spirits. Would you believe it? I have heard of men who will spend forty-five minutes every morning washing, drying, styling, combing, and spraying their hair—and expend no energy in the spirit life. Many women will spend far longer selecting a jogging outfit than they do praying and reading the Bible. We shower and shave. We exercise and energize. We prepare physically but not spiritually. As a pastor I have noticed through the years that many people weep over bodies but not over the spirits of those persons who have gone on. Why? Because we do not have the proper images of ourselves.

Still others of us are more mind- or emotion-conscious than we are spirit-conscious. Moses asked a thought-provoking question, "Who am I?" Let's pause at this juncture and think on that question fraught with eternal meaning. We are spirit-beings. When the Bible declares that God made man in His image, it means that

God is a spirit and "they that worship him must worship him in spirit and in truth" (see Gen. 1:26-27; John 4:24).

Who am I? I am a spirit. I have a soul. I live in a body. If we fed our spirits half as much as our bodies, we would begin to recognize how indescribably valuable we are to God, and consequently a proper self-image would emerge. We lavish ourselves with food, with pleasure, with entertainment, with music, television, and reading. We neglect the spirit. All that can truly feed the spirit is the Word of God and the leadership of the Holy Spirit.

The market is surfeited with books and tapes on self-image. Many of these deal basically with the physical side—*how to dress for success, how to obtain power, how to lose weight,* even *how to slim your tummy.* Dress in stylish clothes, even if those "stylish" clothes make you look like a scarecrow or a clown! Make up correctly. Drive an "in" car. Live in a ritzy condo or town house. Those externals will last for a little while, but they do nothing to build a permanent self-image.

Ho hum. Many other books endeavor to deal with self-image only from the soulish realm. We hear all kinds of advice. "Get hold of your emotions, and don't cry in public." "Learn to laugh and influence others." Ad infinitum. But the truth is we will never have a permanent, positive self-image until we recognize that all of this only touches the outer self. A proper self-image comes from within, and within is the spirit. "Who am I?" I am a spirit. Therefore, I find my real self in the spiritual realm.

Consequently, we are confronted in century twenty with the same question which hounded Moses on the desert: "Who am I?" Let's note first:

An Explanation

Now I recognize that Christians through the centuries have wrestled with the composition of man. Certain thinkers claim that man is soul alone, an indivisible entity, a monad. But the Bible speaks about man being a trichotomy. He is in three parts—spirit, soul, and body. Now I recognize that theologians can discuss and debate the nature of man until the Second Coming. I fully believe from my study of God's Word that we are made up of the outer court (body), the holy place (soul), and the holy of holies (spirit).

We are all too aware of the body. It is visible. We pet and pamper it. Many abuse it with alcohol, drugs, and other immortality. We paint it . . . and tan it. We tone it . . . and attempt to firm it up. We measure it and weigh it. I well remember Stuart Hamblin's hit song, "This Old House." The body is the house God has given us to live in while we sojourn here on planet earth. This aspect of our being deteriorates and disintegrates. It is in the process of decay. One day this body will return to dust.

The soul, I believe, is the seat of our emotions. The soul is not the innermost being. Rather, it is the realm of our emotions.

I repeat: the spirit—the holy of holies—is the innermost being. I equate the spirit with the heart throughout the Bible. "For with the heart man believeth. . ." (see Rom. 10:10). The spirit is that part of us which is going to live as long as God lives—which means your spirit will never die!

Today there are many advocates of the evolutionary process. In other words, man evolved from lower forms. These evolutionists state that man is another animal—more highly developed and more rational, but nonetheless an animal. If such were true, however, there wouldn't be any more wrong with killing a man and eating him than there would be in killing a cow and eating it! What makes a man different is his spirit. It is that part of him which can communicate with God. Animals do not have spirits. There is not a God-like quality in them.

In order to foster the right self-image I need to see that the real me is my spirit. Remember, I am a spirit. I have a soul—I live in my body. With the spirit we contact the spiritual realm. With the soul we contact the emotional realm. With the body we contact the physical realm. The problem is that many are miserable because they look for happiness and peace in the physical realm, in the area of the body. Others seek it in the area of the emotions—the soulish realm. But it is found only in the spirit.

People feel that they can discover happiness through sex or food or even such endeavors as body building, along with aerobics and "pumping iron." Others are miserable in the soulish realm because they look for happiness through aesthetics—music, poetry, prose, intellectual pursuits. But the deepest happiness comes in the spiritual realm. We must ask, "Who am I?" We discover the answer from the Word of God. The real me is a spirit, and the spirit is the only realm where I can find permanent peace and divine direction.

What must we do, then? We must learn to let the new man on the inside of us dominate. When we receive the Lord Jesus Christ and are converted, we turn from a life that has been governed by the physical and/or the mental. Part of us has been dead. Now, in Christ, we are alive spiritually and we need to let the spirit within, activated by the Holy Spirit, dominate. Then and only then can we have the correct self-image. "Who am I?" I am a spirit. I have a soul, and I live in a body. There is not only an explanation, but there is:

An Illustration

In Luke 16 Jesus presents a vivid illustration of man being spirit, soul, and body. Jesus declares:

> 20 And there was a certain rich man, which was clothed in purple and fine linen, and fared sumptuously every day: And there was a certain beggar named Lazarus, which was laid at his gate, full of sores. 21 And desiring to be fed with the crumbs which fell from the rich man's table: moreover the dogs came and

licked his sores. 22 And it came to pass, that the beggar died and was carried by the angels into Abraham's bosom: the rich man also died, and was buried: 23 And in hell he lift up his eyes, being in torment and seeth Abraham afar off, and Lazarus in his bosom. 24 And he cried and said, Father Abraham, have mercy on me, and send Lazarus, that he may dip the tip of his finger in water, and cool my tongue; for I am tormented in this flame. 25 But Abraham said, Son, remember that thou in thy lifetime receivedst thy good things; but now he is comforted, and thou art tormented (vv. 19-25).

The beggar died, but *he* was carried into Abraham's bosom. His body was laid in the grave, but *he* was in the bosom of Abraham, the Hebrew representation of heaven. How? *He* was a spirit!

And we study the plight of the rich man—he was in hades, hell. His spirit and soul were still intact after death. He could still remember; he still had emotion; he was tormented in the flames. He was concerned for his five brothers. When a person dies, he awaits the resurrection of the body. The unsaved like the rich man will be resurrected to corruption. The saved like Lazarus will be resurrected to glorification. In that state prior to the resurrection, the spirit and soul of a person are intact.

Our only means of knowing God is through the spirit. We cannot have a spiritual relationship with Him through human knowledge. To remind you of Jesus' words to the woman at the well, "God is a spirit, and they that worship him must worship him in spirit, and in truth." Naturally, without a relationship of the spirit, man cannot have an intimate knowledge of God. "For the natural man receiveth not the things of the Spirit of God: for they are foolishness unto him: neither can they know them, because they are spiritually discerned" (1 Cor. 2:14). Only through man's spirit, aided by the Holy Spirit of God, can he have a saving standing with God.

"Who am I?" I am a spirit. I have a soul. I live in a body. Finally, I want you to note:

An Application

If all this is true, then one must be in touch with God through one's spirit—as one is energized by the Holy Spirit. I cannot depend on the physical or the emotional aspects in order to have a proper self-image. To have a truly correct image of myself, I must be led and motivated by the Holy Spirit. "For as many as are led by the Spirit of God, they are the sons of God" (Rom. 8:14).

It sounds so simple, doesn't it? But it's true. A person must first be converted to the Lord Jesus Christ. Until then a person is only half alive, and there is no possibility of having the highest self-image of oneself without being in the spiritual realm. You see, a person is not OK until he is OK with Christ. Regardless of what others think, that person is A-OK, because he is OK with God. Then, the self-image, worked upon by the Holy Spirit, begins to shape up to the expectancy of God. So many feel low-down, no count, dirty, filthy, and miserable because of guilt. That guilt is the result of unforgiven, unforsaken, unconfessed sin within the life.

Preston Bailey wrote: "To banish fear you must look within your mind, find the cause of your fear and worry and lack of self-confidence. Then you must train your mental habits to a new point of view. This means substituting faith for fear, a courageous outlook for a lack of self-assurance, a positive attitude toward life for a negative. Fear becomes ingrown only when the fear-bringing situation is not examined and penetrated."

We must be sure of who we are in order to overcome the onslaught of the evil one, the devil. There are three areas of temptation outlined in the Bible. "For all that is in the world, the lust of the flesh, and the lust of the eyes, and the pride of life, is not of the

Father, but is of the world" (1 John 2:16). The appeals of this wicked world system entice through the temptations of the soul and the body. The body can become boss, and then preoccupation with sex or weight or pastimes dominates us. And the devil is not satisfied to tempt our bodies and souls. He loves to work on one's spirit.

"The devil made me do it." No, he didn't really. You and I cooperated with him. We are prone to blame the devil for what actually belongs to our flesh. We simply let the body rule us. Many of us do not want to accept the responsibility if we can blame it on demons.

How are we to overcome? How are we to build a proper self-image? If the temptation comes from the world, it attacks the soul. Consequently we have to overcome through *faith*. First John 5:4 states it plainly: "For whatsoever is born of God overcometh the world: and this is the victory that overcometh the world, even our faith." Ah, there's the key. *Faith*.

How appropriate are the inspiring words of John Greenleaf Whittier:

> Nothing before, nothing behind;
>   The steps of faith
> Fall on the seeming void, and find
>   The Rock beneath.

If the temptation comes from the flesh, it is against the body. We overcome here through *fleeing*. First Corinthians 6:18, for instance, admonishes: "Flee fornication. Every sin that a man doeth is without the body; but he that committeth fornication sinneth against his own body." We are not to fight this temptation—we are to flee it! Run for cover beneath the shadow of the Almighty.

If the temptation comes from the devil, it is certainly against the spirit. Here we are not to faith it or to flee it—we are to *fight* it. Paul aptly wrote: "For we wrestle not against flesh and blood, but against principalities, against powers, against the rulers of the darkness of this world, against spiritual wickedness in high places" (Eph. 6:12).

And James gave this command: "Submit yourselves to God, resist the devil, and he will flee from you" (4:7). You are not supposed to run from the devil—he is supposed to run from you! The blood of Jesus Christ, God's exalted Son, has already conquered the devil!

Now how are we to move forward? One must be tuned to his spirit and not to the body or even his soul. We must not make decisions in life on the basis of the physical or the soulish. We should never decide because "we feel like it." We should make our decisions from the spirit through the Holy Spirit. How are we to be led by the Spirit?

It is so rudimentary, so elementary—and we have heard it again and again. Withdraw with the Word. Feast on it. Meditate on it. Drink it in. Remember the prayer of the psalmist to God: "Thy word have I hid in mine heart, that I might not sin against thee" (Ps. 119:11). "Thy word is a lamp unto my feet, and a light unto my path" (Ps. 119:105). Cherish the Word. Let it speak. Pray as though everything depended on it. Hear Paul as he wrote to his beloved brethren at Philippi:

> Be careful [anxious] for nothing; but in every thing by prayer
> and supplication with thanksgiving let your requests be made
> known unto God" (Phil. 4:6).

And it wouldn't hurt most of us to fast for a period—a day, two, three. Remember that "faith cometh by hearing, and hearing by the word of God" (Rom. 10:17). Search deep inside and ask the Holy Spirit to purge your spirit—and your body and your soul—from every sin and negative influence of the devil. After all, the devil wants you to have a bad self-image, Christian. He can render your testimony ineffective if you spend a goodly portion of your time feeling bad about yourself and lamenting, "I'm no good. I'm so dirty and filthy. I've always hated myself." That's the devil's lie. He wants you, Christian, to live as though you had never been converted, never been saved—as though you have never had an encounter with the beautiful Lord Jesus Christ. Remember this: the devil—Satan, Lucifer, Beelzebub—wants you to have an abysmally low view of yourself.

Spend more time with the spirit than you do with the body. Budget your time. All of us should devote more energy and time to the spirit than to the body. Spiritual exercise is necessary, or you will lose "tone" in the spirit life. You will become flabby and weak.

"Who am I?" I am a spirit. I have a soul. I live in a body. How do I image myself? I am indescribably valuable to God. You and I are worth more than a king's ransom to God. Only when you realize your worth to God can you begin to build a positive self-image. Hear me. Through Christ, you can begin to become the beautiful you God intends.

Many will never develop a decent self-image until they come alive spiritually. If you have never received Christ, your self-image will always be faulty and tarnished. You will be in the pits in this life—and in "the pit" in eternity! Come to Jesus for "His cleansing power." Turn over your negative life to His positive, saving grace. Let Him transform you and translate you into "the kingdom of his dear Son." See yourself as one for whom Christ came and died to redeem, and self-image will begin to develop.

After an interlude, back to Moses. It is hardly essential for me to mention that backward, timid Moses became the leader of a mighty nation, guiding them out of Egyptian bondage and then to the Promised Land, even though he himself "saw it afar." Moses realized that God had a mission for him. This was the same man who stammered and stumbled, mumbled and moped. The same man who asked, "Who am I?" And he meant, "Who, little old me?" Who was on the Mount of Transfiguration with Jesus (besides Peter, James, and John, of course)? Moses and Elijah, and they were transfigured along with our glorious Lord Jesus.

Moses finally began to realize he was the servant and emancipator of God. Only he could do exactly what God wanted. And he didn't have to do it all by himself. God gave him Aaron who was fluent and could help serve as Moses' occasional spokesman.

Do you feel worthless? Pitiful? Of no account? Many do. But you must determine right now who you are. Many Christian psychologists will follow this line of thinking with clients who are ambivalent. They will ask, "Now, what do you want to be? Better still, *who* do you want to be? Do you want to be the flirtatious 'dirty ole man' or 'the servant of God'?" Or "do you want to be 'the social climber' or 'the soul-winner'?" In other words, who are you?

You will never move toward a proper self-image as long as you trust in the physical realm. In the final analysis, neither money nor status are the determining factors in self-image. The quality and worth of the person are. You must move to the core of the matter—the spirit deep within, the holy of holies in your life. You will never have a permanent, positive self-image until you move past the outer realm and plunge into the real you—the spiritual part.

All of this is bound up in becoming "the express image" of the Master. Only then will you have a winning self-image. "Christ in you, the hope of glory."

We have come once again to the end of a volume. It could be the beginning of a whole new way of life . . . *tracing the rainbow through the rain.*

Notes

Chapter 3
  1. Ida Nelle Hollaway, *Loneliness: The Untapped Resource* (Nashville: Broadman Press, 1982), p. 34.
  2. From *The Hills Beyond* (New York: Harper Brothers, 1941), p. 186.
  3. Velma Darbo Stevens, *A Fresh Look at Loneliness* (Nashville: Broadman Press, 1981), pp. 9-10.
  4. Hollaway, Ibid., pp. 75-76.

Chapter 6
  1. Leonard Cammer, M.D., *Up from Depression* (New York: Pocket Books, 1974), pp. 4-5.
  2. Ralph Speas, *How to Deal with How You Feel* (Nashville: Broadman Press, 1980), p. 23.
  3. Nelson L. Price, *Farewell to Fear* (Nashville: Broadman Press, 1983), pp. 112-113.
  4. Price, Ibid., p. 17.
  5. Brooks R. Faulkner, *Burnout in Ministry* (Nashville: Broadman Press, 1981), p. 11.
  6. Hardy R. Denham, Jr., *Freedom from Frustration* (Nashville: Broadman Press, 1981), pp. 33,37.